MONTANA
WILDLIFE
VIEWING
GUIDE

Carol and Hank Fischer

FALCON PRESS

PUBLIC LAND MANAGEMENT AGENCIES IN MONTANA

The U.S. Department of Agriculture Forest Service, Northern Region, manages 10 national forests containing 16.7 million acres, 18 percent of all lands in Montana. USFS lands are located throughout the state, although most are in western Montana. National forests were established on conservation principles— the wise use of natural resources. Congress has mandated that national forests be managed for multiple use, allowing for a combination of uses that best serve the public interest.

Bureau of Land Management administers 8.2 million acres of public lands in Montana, nearly 10 percent of the state. Most BLM lands are in eastern Montana. The BLM's mandate for multiple-use management requires that resources be administered in a combination that will best meet the present and future needs of the American public.

The Montana Department of Fish, Wildlife and Parks manages 389,000 acres, including 11 state parks, 80 recreation areas, 20 monuments, 62 wildlife management areas, and over 200 fishing access sites. The land managed by the MDFWP is dispersed throughout the state. The MDFWP is charged with the responsibility for managing Montana's fish, wildlife, and recreational resources, and for providing optimum outdoor recreational opportunities for Montanans and visitors.

The U.S. Fish and Wildlife Service administers 1.1 million acres in Montana that include 20 wildlife refuges, 10 waterfowl production areas, and three fish hatcheries (one percent of Montana lands) Its mission is to conserve, protect, and enhance fish and wildlife and their habitats for the continuing benefit of the American people.

The Montana Department of State Lands owns 5.1 million acres in Montana (5.5 percent of Montana lands). Approximately two-thirds of the land is east of the Continental Divide. The state was originally granted two sections in each township in its enabling legislation to support public schools. Many of these sections have since been traded to gain larger blocks of state lands. The DSL has four major missions: trust land management, wildfire suppression, mined land reclamation, and forestry assistance.

The National Park Service manages 1.2 million acres in Montana including two national parks, one national monument, one national battlefield, one national recreation area, and two national historic sites. The NPS was established to preserve and protect resources unimpaired for future generations while providing for public use and enjoyment.

Design, typesetting, and other prepress work by Falcon Press, Helena, Montana
Printed in Singapore

Library of Congress Number 90-080041
ISBN 1-56044-001-5

Front cover photo: Mountain goat by Michael S. Sample
Habitat artwork on pages 14-21 by René Eisenbart

CONTENTS

Primary funding for the research and development of this book was provided by:
  USDA Forest Service, Northern Region
  Bureau of Land Management
  Montana Department of Fish, Wildlife and Parks
  U.S. Fish and Wildlife Service
  Montana Department of State Lands
  U.S. Bureau of Reclamation
  Travel Montana/Montana Department of Commerce
  Defenders of Wildlife
  Len and Sandy Sargent
  Bob and Hopie Stevens

Other important contributors include:
  The Nature Conservancy
  Patagonia, Inc.
  Upper Missouri Breaks and
    Yellowstone Valley Audubon Chapters

Project Coordinator
  Defenders of Wildlife

VIEWING WILDLIFE

This guide was designed for both the casual and the serious wildlife viewer. We expect it will be valuable to birders, wildlife photographers, and families seeking an interesting outing. Our emphasis on different types of access to wildlife-watching sites should make this book of special interest to hikers, boaters, skiers, and bicyclists as well as recreational-vehicle owners and auto tourers. We also made a special effort to underscore wildlife viewing opportunities for the physically challenged. Finally, we have emphasized wildlife viewing opportunities that are close to Montana's largest towns.

Some sites offer more reliable wildlife viewing than others, which can be a function both of the population density of a species and of its habits. For instance, waterfowl can be seen more predictably than great horned owls or pileated woodpeckers, just as prairie dogs are more dependable than beaver or coyotes. Be sure to keep in mind that wildlife viewing at some sites may be much better at particular times of the year. This rule is especially true for migrating shorebirds and waterfowl, and for such species as sage grouse or sharp-tailed grouse, which congregate for mating in the spring.

But once you're sure you're looking at the right place at the right time, the single most important way to increase your chances of seeing wildlife is to go early—right at dawn. This is almost always the best time, with dusk being a close second. An attempt at wildlife viewing during the heat of a summer day is usually a prescription for disappointment.

The only equipment that's really important for wildlife watching is a pair of binoculars, although a field guide can be helpful. A spotting scope can be fun to use but heavy if you're doing much hiking. The real keys are to go to the right place at the right time, to be there early, and to be patient.

Carol and Hank Fischer

HOW TO USE THIS BOOK

The **color strips** on the outside of the pages are keyed to each of the six tourist regions and two national parks in Montana. The sites are numbered consecutively from 1 to 113, with all sites in a region placed together and numbered from north to south. Maps of each region with the site numbers can be found at the beginning of each section.

Symbols of animals and plants are limited to four per site and indicate either the species most likely to be present or those unique to the area.

The **site descriptions** first describe the habitat and then identify some of the species found at the site. Only unique or representative species are listed, not every species at the site.

Directions given are based on the Official Montana Highway Map. Forest, county, and local roads are described from Bureau of Land Management or U.S. Forest Service maps. Only towns named on the Official Montana Highway Map are listed as the **closest town.**

Facilities are listed only if they are on the site. In some cases, rest rooms or hotels may be nearby.

Ownership signifies the agency or entity that either owns or manages the site. The names of private owners or organizations are not always listed. Private sites have been included in this book only with the permission of the landowners. Please respect their rights when visiting these sites.

The **phone number** listed after ownership is the number to use if you have questions concerning individual sites. This is usually the managing agency or individual. Unless otherwise noted, all phone numbers are in Montana, area code 406.

Recreational icons are listed to indicate various opportunities at each site. Some sites may only have one icon.

TRAVEL INFORMATION

For additional Montana travel information, contact Travel Montana, Department of Commerce, 1424 9th Ave., Helena, MT 59604, phone 1-800-541-1447 (in Montana, call 444-2654).

MAP INFORMATION

Montana is divided into the six major regions shown on this map. Wildlife viewing sites are numbered consecutively in a general pattern from west to east. Each region forms a separate section in this book, and each section begins with a detailed map of that region. In addition, maps are included with the sections on Glacier and Yellowstone national parks.

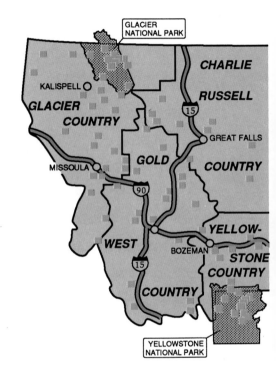

SITE OWNERSHIP ABBREVIATIONS

USFWS—U.S. Fish and Wildlife Service
MDFWP—Montana Department of Fish, Wildlife and Parks
USFS—USDA Forest Service
BLM—Bureau of Land Management
NPS—National Park Service
BuRec—Bureau of Reclamation
ACE—U.S. Army Corps of Engineers
DSL—Department of State Lands
PVT—Private

FEATURED WILDLIFE

 Songbirds

 Upland birds

 Waterfowl

 Shorebirds

 Wading birds

 Birds of prey

 Small mammals

 Hoofed mammals

 Carnivores

 Freshwater mammals

 Fish

 Reptiles, amphibians

 Insects

 Wildflowers

FACILITIES

P
Parking

 Restrooms

 Lodging

$
Entry fee

 Accessible to persons with disabilities

 Restaurant

 Boat ramp

A
Campground

 Picnic

RECREATION OPPORTUNITIES

 Hiking

 Bicycling

 Cross-country skiing

 Small boats

 Large boats

HIGHWAY SIGNS

Wildlife Viewing Area

As you travel across Montana, look for these special highway signs that identify wildlife viewing sites. Most signs show the binoculars logo or the words "Wildlife Viewing Area," with an arrow pointing toward the site.

State of Montana
Office of the Governor
Helena, Montana 59620
406-444-3111

STAN STEPHENS
GOVERNOR

Dear Reader,

Montana's abundant wildlife resource is one of our state's many attractions. It is more common than not to hear people, Montanans and visitors, alike, say that one of the reasons they are in Montana is the unique opportunity it provides to view elk, deer and antelope roaming freely across our wide open spaces.

The diversity of Montana's wildlife population is almost unsurpassed. We offer some of the finest wildlife viewing in North America. The nation's largest bighorn sheep herd resides here. Snow geese gather by the thousands. Hundreds of bald eagles can be viewed congregating along our rivers and lakes during various seasons of the year. We have bison, mountain goats, wild horses, prairie dogs and the last remaining grizzly bear population in the lower 48 states. We have wildness -- often only a short distance from our paved highways.

The treasures Montana offers the wildlife viewer is chronicled in this publication, Montana's Wildlife Viewing Guide. Private organizations and public agencies have joined to create an outstanding book which informs you about Montana's wildlife populations, and shows you where to view them.

There are approximately 115 viewing sites listed within these pages. Some of the sites are within Glacier and Yellowstone National Parks. Outside the parks, the viewing areas are marked by road signs at their actual locations along the state's highway. All provide you with excellent viewing opportunities.

Get to know the wonders of Big Sky Country. Follow this guide and you'll be sure to see and experience the best of what Montana has to offer.

Enjoy the view,

STAN STEPHENS
Governor

Defenders
OF WILDLIFE

From all indications, wildlife watching may become the premier outdoor recreation activity of the 1990s. At a time when participation in hunting has gradually declined—except in Montana—the number of adult Americans involved in wildlife watching and related activities has increased tremendously—one federal survey reports a sixty-nine per cent increase between 1980 and 1985.

But there's bad news and good news in this apparent shift in wildlife constituencies. For the last century, state wildlife conservation programs have been funded primarily by sportsmen, both through license fees and through excise taxes on the equipment they use—guns, ammunition, fishing rods, etc. So, the bad news is that decreasing numbers of sportsmen will mean less money for state wildlife conservation programs.

The good news is that there has been no decrease in the total number of people concerned about wildlife. To the contrary, with the burgeoning numbers of nonconsumptive users—and it should be noted that many people who hunt and fish are also interested in birdwatching and wildlife photography—the total number of people involved in wildlife-related recreation has increased significantly.

The real challenge for the 1990s is to develop programs that allow the nonhunting public to make a larger contribution to wildlife conservation. All of us—hunters and nonhunters alike—want to protect habitat, prevent species from becoming endangered, and recover species which are in trouble. All people concerned about wildlife should be willing to help pay the bills. But we must take that willingness one step further. We must assume responsibility for developing new conservation programs, geared toward the entire public, that will guarantee we have wildlife to watch into the next century. Defenders of Wildlife will strive to be a major voice of this wildlife-viewing public.

Dr. Rupert Cutler
President
Defenders of Wildlife

Dr. Rupert Cutler, watching bison in Yellowstone National Park.

Montana contains a magnificent array of wildlife, such as this trumpeter swan on its nest at Red Rock Lakes National Wildlife Refuge. The abundance and diversity of wildlife in Montana provides excellent wildlife viewing at more than 100 sites all across the state. MICHAEL S. SAMPLE

INTRODUCTION

When Montana's first official explorers, Lewis and Clark, passed through what was then part of the Louisiana Purchase in 1805-06, they were literally struck silent by the numbers and diversity of wildlife. Captain Clark was so awed that at one point in his journal he vowed to write no further about this country's amazing animal numbers for fear no one would believe him.

Montana's magnificent wildlife continues to amaze and delight visitors. Consider a few of Montana's superlatives:

- It has the largest migratory elk herd in the nation (Northern Yellowstone Winter Range).
- It has the largest breeding population of trumpeter swans in the lower U.S. (Red Rock Lakes National Wildlife Refuge).
- It claims the spot where more golden eagles have been seen in a single day than anywhere else in the country (Rocky Mountain Front Eagle Migration Area).
- It has the largest population of nesting common loons in the western United States (Clearwater Chain-of-Lakes Loon Driving Tour).
- It has the largest native herd of Rocky Mountain bighorn sheep in the U.S. (Sun River Canyon).
- It has the largest grizzly bear population south of Canada.
- It has the largest population of gray wolves west of the Mississippi.

Montana has more elk, deer, and pronghorn antelope than it does people. The average square mile of land in Montana contains 1.4 elk, 1.4 pronghorn antelope, and 3.3 deer. That same Montana square mile contains fewer than five people. When you compare that number to population densities for some other states—Colorado (27.9), Washington (62.1), New York (370.6), and New Jersey (986.2)—it's clear that Montana has more wildlife and fewer people than anywhere else in the contiguous United States.

Besides elk, deer, and pronghorn antelope, Montana has a great deal of other wildlife—more than 500 species of mammals, birds, reptiles, and amphibians. Most of these species can be seen by the average person with little more than a pair of binoculars. For instance:

- At Freezeout Lake Wildlife Management Area one can see as many as 300,000 snow geese and 10,000 tundra swans during migration.
- At Bowdoin National Wildlife Refuge it's possible to see up to 1,700 nesting pelicans.
- At the magnificent Lewis and Clark Caverns you can see a maternity colony of big-eared bats.
- At the KooKooSint Sheep Viewing Area you can get close-up views of bighorn sheep.
- At Bad Pass Trail you may see one of the nation's few remaining herds of wild horses.
- At the Kootenai River it's possible to see up to 175 bald eagles on a single fall day.
- Near The Pines Recreation Area one can see as many as 100 sage grouse performing their extraordinary spring mating rituals.
- At Lost Creek State Park mountain goats are readily viewed, with easy access.
- At Greycliff Prairie Dog Town one can predictably see large numbers of prairie dogs and learn about their interesting ecology through some exceptional environ mental education displays.
- At the National Bison Range one can find some of the best opportunities in the country to photograph bison, blue grouse, bighorn sheep, and antelope.

Montana is probably best known for its two national parks—Glacier and Yellowstone. Glacier National Park is fully within Montana; Yellowstone National Park is shared with Wyoming and Idaho.

Glacier is particularly renowned for its mountain goats and bighorn sheep. The Walton Goat Lick Overlook and the Going-to-the-Sun Road are exceptional spots for seeing mountain goats, and Many Glacier and Cracker Lake are good places to view bighorns. But Glacier is probably best known for its remarkable grizzly bear population—denser than anywhere else in the lower 48 states. Grizzlies are often seen at Many Glacier or along the Highline Trek. Check with park officials for the best ways to view grizzly bears safely. Glacier Park is also the site of a small population of gray wolves. While wolves are seldom viewed, tracks can sometimes be seen and on rare occasions the wolves can be heard near Big Prairie.

Yellowstone Park is famous not only for its diversity of wildlife, but for its abundance as well. It has as dense a population of large ungulates—elk, bison, moose, and deer—as any place in North America. It has frequently been called the American equivalent of Africa's Serengeti. The spectacular Lamar and Hayden valleys are the best places to view these large grazing animals. Grizzly bears are also present in Yellowstone; Antelope Creek is a great place for safe viewing. The Seven Mile Bridge is a premier spot for watching trumpeter swans, and the Grand Canyon of the Yellowstone is an exceptional place to watch nesting osprey.

The only drawback to wildlife viewing in Glacier and Yellowstone is that the parks can be crowded in the summer (although you can avoid the crowds by getting up early or by visiting in the fall, winter, or spring). The good news is that many of the non-park sites listed in this book have similar wildlife viewing opportunities without the crowds.

Nowhere is this more true than in eastern Montana, where the prairie grasslands and rugged draws offer remarkable wildlife viewing in relative solitude. The expansive Charles M. Russell National Wildlife Refuge (at more than a million acres, it's the third largest refuge in the lower 48) probably contains the wildest remaining habitats of the Northern Great Plains. It has a prairie elk herd, bighorn sheep, prairie dogs, turkeys, and both sharp-tailed and sage grouse. Makoshika State Park, a spectacular badlands area, has a notable congregation of turkey vultures and is a great place to find horned lizards and bull snakes. At the Terry Badlands, you can almost always see golden eagles. The Manning Corral Prairie Dog Town is a 1,000-acre area where you can not only see prairie dogs, but also predators including coyotes, badgers, and ferruginous hawks. Then there's the seldom-visited Medicine Lake National Wildlife Refuge, where one can see thousands of nesting pelicans, grebes performing their mating rituals, and as many as 100,000 ducks and geese during migration.

Wildlife viewing in western Montana generally takes place in mountainous terrain or in the broad valleys that dissect the mountains. The Ninepipe National Wildlife Refuge offers terrific birding for waterfowl, shorebirds, and raptors. Wild Horse Island in Flathead Lake offers unparalleled opportunities to see not only wild horses, but also bighorn sheep and bald eagles in pristine surroundings. At the Skalkaho Game Preserve one can always hear elk bugling in the fall. At Red Rock Lakes National Wildlife Refuge one can watch sandhill cranes perform their ungainly mating rituals, and the area has an extraordinary concentration of hawks and eagles. Freezeout Lake Wildlife Management Area offers what may be the highest concentration of shorebirds (yellowlegs, avocets, willets) anywhere in the state.

This book also includes some unusual, nontraditional wildlife viewing sites. Several fish hatcheries are listed because they present exceptional opportunities to view fish and to learn more about Montana's fisheries. They're great places for family outings or school groups. Giant Springs State Park and the Creston Fish Hatchery are highly recommended, especially during spawning times. Some outstanding wildlife museums have been included; the Rocky Mountain Elk Foundation Visitor Center in Missoula is a must for people with a consuming interest in elk. We have also included a butterfly viewing site (Jimmy Joe Campground) and a unique restaurant (Broad Axe Lodge and Restaurant) where you can watch elk and bighorn sheep while eating dinner.

Wildlife viewing is a recreational pursuit that's becoming increasingly popular among persons with disabilities—those with hearing, sight, or mobility problems. While most of the sites in the book are accessible by automobiles, we have highlighted viewing areas where agencies have made special efforts to help people with special needs (check the facilities icons). We have listed areas that either have trails that can accommodate wheelchairs, or that have bathroom or picnic facilities designed for the physically challenged. These include some exceptional sites. The Sheepshead Mountain Recreation Area has nature trails, picnic facilities, and even a fishing area—all designed to allow those with limited mobility to enjoy the outdoors. Palisade Falls is a 0.6-mile paved nature trail with interpretive signs written in Braille, that winds through a beautiful forest to a spectacular waterfall. The National Bison Range also merits special mention for its unique environmental education program for the disabled.

Finally, this book has also identified more than a dozen "urban" wildlife viewing sites. These are great places for people who want to see wildlife but can't travel far, for out-of-town visitors who lack the time for a major outing, and school groups looking for good areas for field trips.

Great Falls' Giant Springs State Park has a fish hatchery, a wildlife museum, and an exceptional trail along the Missouri River, where several species of gulls and waterfowl as well as bald eagles typically occur. Kirk Hill, a couple of miles from Bozeman, is an outstanding birding area (over 70 species recorded) where the Museum of the Rockies has developed interpretive signs that identify wildflowers and trees. Only two miles from downtown Missoula, Kelly Island is an outstanding natural area featuring waterfowl, beaver, bald eagles, and a great blue heron rookery. In Billings next to the Yellowstone River lies Two Moon Park, where more than 200 species of birds have been identified, including white pelicans, wood ducks, bald eagles, and screech owls. Near Havre is little-known Beaver Creek County Park, which at 10,000 acres may be the largest county park in the United States. It's a great place for birding and a reliable spot to see coyotes, eagles, and lots of deer.

COMBINING WILDLIFE VIEWING WITH OTHER OUTDOOR RECREATION

Since so many people combine wildlife viewing with other outdoor recreation, we have made a special effort to develop viewing sites that are accessible by a variety of means—from a car, on foot, from a boat, on a bike, etc. Each viewing site has special icons that identify modes of access. These include symbols for hiking, boating (small or large craft), bicycling, and cross-country skiing.

We have included several sites where good wildlife viewing is possible just from your automobile. The Clearwater Chain-of-Lakes Loon Driving Tour is such a place, and the book lists several other auto routes.

At some sites, quality wildlife viewing is possible only by walking. The mile-long hike to the top of Square Butte (a Montana landmark) to see mountain goats and eagles is one good example; or a walk on Howery's Island (along the Yellowstone River) is another.

The Clearwater Canoe Trail—which offers exceptional viewing of waterfowl and bald eagles—is an outstanding small boat trip, as is the 149-mile float down the Missouri River, part of the National Wild and Scenic River System. A good large boat trip is the tour boat trip through the Gates of the Mountains, where you can see bighorn sheep and mountain goats.

Cross-country skiing can be another great way to view wildlife, though special care must be taken not to harass wild animals on their winter ranges. Both Yellowstone and Glacier Parks have some exceptional opportunities, as does the Sun River Canyon and the Mount Haggin Wildlife Management Area.

Finally, bicycling can be an outstanding way to see wildlife. While many roads on national forests or on state wildlife management areas are closed to motorized use at certain times of the year, they remain open to mountain biking. Places such as the Skalkaho Game Preserve, the Blackfoot-Clearwater Wildlife Management Area, the UL Bend National Wildlife Refuge, and the Beaver Creek County Park offer great opportunities to exercise and see wildlife at the same time.

Responsible wildlife viewing means not interferring with animals as they go about their normal lives. In this case, a bull elk intent on following other elk passes a wildlife photographer, who wisely stays out of the way. NEAL AND MARY JANE MISHLER

RESPONSIBLE WILDLIFE VIEWING

While it seems strange to think wildlife could be watched to death, constant harassment can harm wild animals. At most of the wildlife viewing sites in this book, rules are posted that explain where people can go and when. It's critical that wildlife watchers obey the rules and make sure others obey them as well. It's especially important for wildlife viewers to stay within designated areas and on specified trails. Many wildlife species can adapt to human use—even heavy human use—if people's movements are routine and predictable. The important thing is that animals are allowed to carry out their normal behavior without interruption.

You know you're approaching too close when animals stop feeding, when they stand up after they've been resting, when they change their direction of travel, or most obviously, when they turn and start moving away. People who care about wildlife should understand some of the consequences of approaching animals too closely or too persistently:

- the animals might be startled into traffic where they could be hit by vehicles.
- mothers and their young might become separated.
- a human scent track might lead predators to a nest or to young.
- the animals might be distracted from their predators.
- incubating or breeding birds could be kept off their nests, resulting in chilled eggs or young.
- disturbing animals in the winter may cause animals to use up valuable energy at a time when they are already severely stressed by winter cold and limited food supplies.

Be sure not to pick up any wild baby animals. They are usually not orphaned or abandoned—their parents typically know exactly where the young animals are and will return and feed them. It is illegal to take home wild animals. Furthermore, sick or injured animals may bite or carry infectious diseases.

Finally, it's important to understand that approaching wildlife too closely is dangerous, especially with large mammals such as bison, moose, and black or grizzly bears.

DON'T FEED THE ANIMALS

You undoubtedly know that feeding wildlife can put you and your friends in danger. But many people are unaware just how harmful feeding can be to the animals. Consider these points:

- Animals that receive roadside handouts tend to frequent such areas, resulting in a higher probability of their being hit by vehicles.
- Animals that become accustomed to human food typically are unable to discern good food from aluminum, plastic, or other wrappings that can seriously harm their digestive systems.
- Animals that become accustomed to human food may become aggressive around humans; the result is that they must be removed or killed.
- Animals that hibernate or migrate can be particularly harmed by unnatural food sources.
- Animals that hibernate may not gain sufficient body weight to survive the winter, while animals that migrate may not start their trips early enough.

WESTERN TANAGER

COOPERS HAWK

DOUGLAS-FIR

CONIFEROUS FOREST

Found especially in western Montana, this forested habitat—which covers approximately 30 percent of the state—is typically associated with mountains.

AMERICAN ELK

INDIAN PAINTBRUSH

TRILLIUM

TAILED FROG

WESTERN HEMLOCK

RED SQUIRREL

PINE MARTEN

PILEATED WOODPECKER

LUPINE

EADOW VOLE

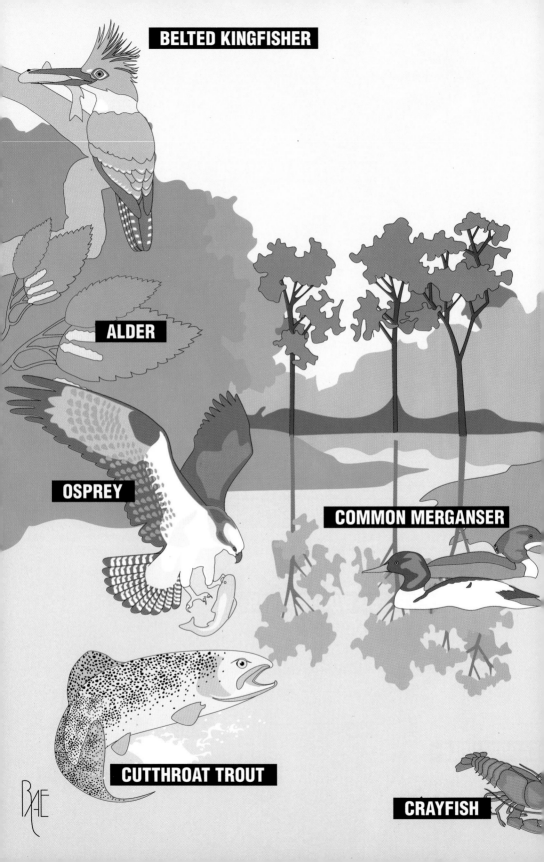

BELTED KINGFISHER

ALDER

OSPREY

COMMON MERGANSER

CUTTHROAT TROUT

CRAYFISH

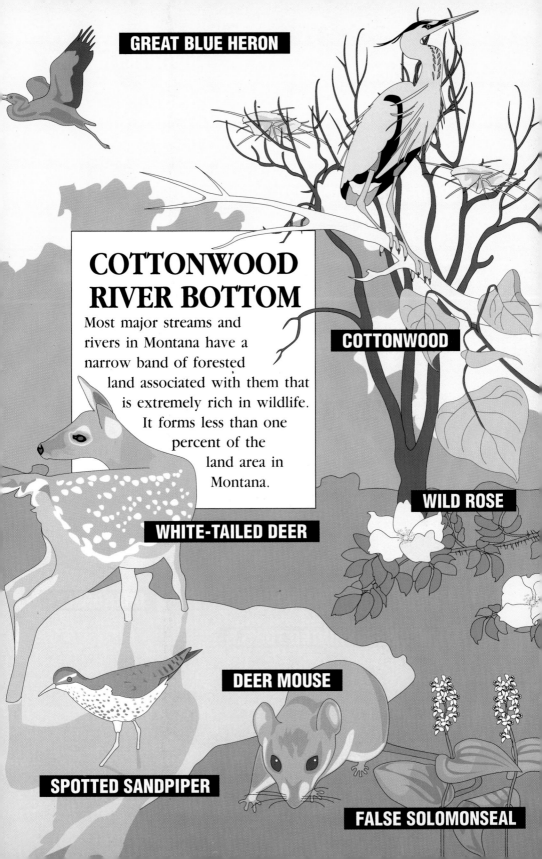

GREAT BLUE HERON

COTTONWOOD RIVER BOTTOM

Most major streams and rivers in Montana have a narrow band of forested land associated with them that is extremely rich in wildlife. It forms less than one percent of the land area in Montana.

COTTONWOOD

WILD ROSE

WHITE-TAILED DEER

DEER MOUSE

SPOTTED SANDPIPER

FALSE SOLOMONSEAL

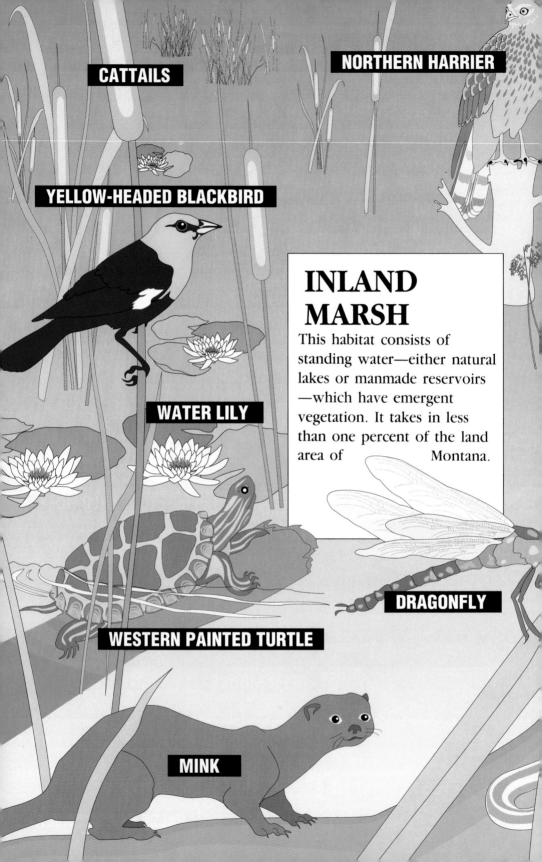

CATTAILS

NORTHERN HARRIER

YELLOW-HEADED BLACKBIRD

INLAND MARSH

This habitat consists of standing water—either natural lakes or manmade reservoirs —which have emergent vegetation. It takes in less than one percent of the land area of Montana.

WATER LILY

DRAGONFLY

WESTERN PAINTED TURTLE

MINK

VIOLET-GREEN SWALLOWS

PINTAIL DUCK

BULRUSHES

BEAVER

MUSKRAT

AVOCET

WESTERN GARTER SNAKE

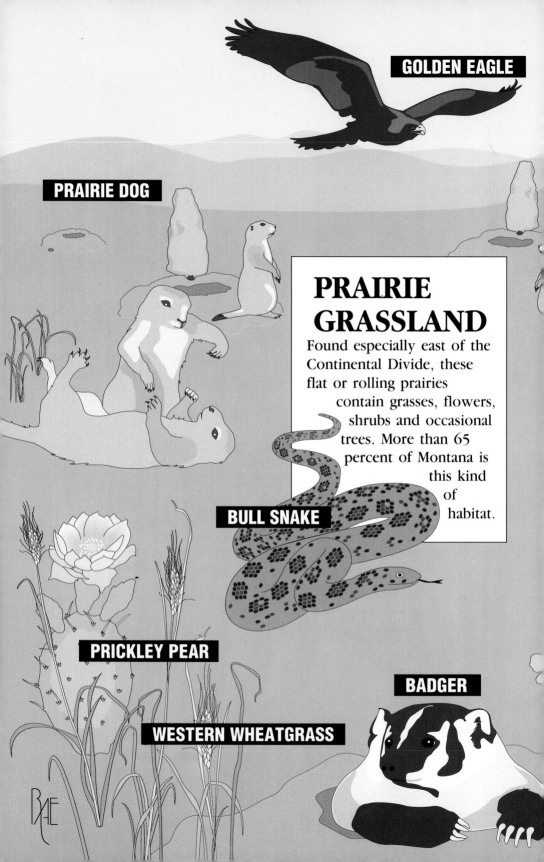

GOLDEN EAGLE

PRAIRIE DOG

PRAIRIE GRASSLAND

Found especially east of the Continental Divide, these flat or rolling prairies contain grasses, flowers, shrubs and occasional trees. More than 65 percent of Montana is this kind of habitat.

BULL SNAKE

PRICKLEY PEAR

BADGER

WESTERN WHEATGRASS

PRONGHORN

SHARP-TAILED GROUSE

BURROWING OWL

BLUE GRAMA

BIG SAGEBRUSH

WESTERN MEADOWLARK

YELLOW EVENING PRIMROSE

1 **Vinal Creek**
2 **Murphy Lake**
3 **Kootenai River**
4 **KooKooSint Sheep Viewing Area**
5 **Smith Lake Waterfowl Production Area**
6 **Creston National Fish Hatchery**
7 **Wild Horse Island**
8 **Swan River National Wildlife Refuge**
9 **Old Squeezer Loop Road**
10 **Ninepipe National Wildlife Refuge and State Wildlife Management Area**
11 **National Bison Range**
12 **Clearwater Canoe Trail**
13 **Clearwater Chain-of-Lakes Loon Driving Tour**
14 **Blackfoot-Clearwater Wildlife Management Area**
15 **Kelly Island**
16 **Rocky Mountain Elk Foundation Wildlife Visitor Center**
17 **Greenough Park**
18 **Lee Metcalf National Wildlife Refuge**
19 **Skalkaho Game Preserve**
20 **Broad Axe Lodge and Restaurant**

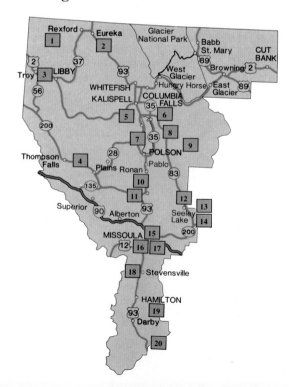

1 — Vinal Creek

Description: The moist coastal weather in this part of the Kootenai National Forest has created impressive old-growth timber stands. The first four miles of the trail along Vinal Creek pass through a stand of western larch (tamarack), some four feet or more in diameter and most over 300 years old. At the creek crossing, there are huge red cedars, some more than 25 feet around, providing habitat for pileated woodpeckers, barred owls, goshawks, and numerous warblers, vireos, and kinglets. The trail splits near the 28-foot Turner Falls; the uphill fork goes to Mount Henry while the other leads to a chain of five lakes (Fish Lakes) in a narrow canyon. Along the Fish Lakes trail (#397), look for deer and moose. Waterfowl can be seen in the marshy areas, while common loons and great blue herons are sometimes seen. The rocky canyon is a good place to see and hear pikas (rock rabbits). The fairly level trail is good for cross-country skiing and viewing deer and elk in the winter. Be aware, however, that Forest Road 746 is typically plowed only to within one mile of the trail head.

Directions: Take Secondary 508 to Yaak, then follow FS Road 746 for five miles northeast of the town (this road parallels the east side of the upper Yaak River). The well-marked trail begins just north of a bridge that crosses Vinal Creek.

Ownership: USFS (293-6211)
Size: Six miles

P

2 — Murphy Lake

Description: This small lake is in a heavily forested area with adjacent marshland. A series of four signs describes the loons that nest here and their habitat. Nesting loons are very sensitive, and signed buoys mark areas closed to the public. Canoeists can see horned grebes, waterfowl, bald eagles, an active heron rookery, nesting osprey, and beavers. Much of the land north of Murphy Lake is key winter range for white-tailed and mule deer. A signed cross-country ski trail off of FS Road 7008 passes through this range, where moose are also occasionally spotted.

Directions: From Eureka, follow U.S. 93 for 14 miles southeast, then take FS Road 7008 at the northwest corner of Murphy Lake. Follow this road to the picnic area and the loon information signs.

Ownership: USFS (882-4451)
Size: 200 acres **Closest Town:** Eureka

 Even though riparian areas make up less than one-half of one-percent of Montana's land area, fully one-half of the state's bird species nest only in these streamside areas.

3 Kootenai River

Description: This beautiful large mountain river is outstanding for viewing bald eagles, nesting osprey, great blue herons, and waterfowl. From the Alexander Creek Picnic Area, look across the river and watch bald eagles and osprey (more than twenty nests between Libby and the dam) diving for fish and returning to nearby snags. In the fall, bald eagles concentrate below the dam to catch kokanee salmon. Over 160 bald eagles have been sighted in one day. Eagle migration starts around the first week in October, peaks around the first week in November, and tapers off around mid-December. In March, large waterfowl concentrations pass through. The Corps of Engineers has placed goose nesting platforms on the river's east side. A river float between Libby Dam and the town of Libby is an excellent way to view raptors and waterfowl.

Directions: From Libby, take Montana 37 for 13.5 miles to Forest Road 228 (just before the bridge over the Kootenai River), which runs along the west side of the river. Follow this road until you reach Powerhouse Road, where you can launch a boat, view from the Alexander Creek Picnic Area, or continue driving along this road to the dam. Floaters can take-out at the old bridge abutments, about eight miles down river from the dam, or at Libby, 17 miles down river.

Ownership: PVT, USFS, ACE (293-5577)
Size: 17 miles **Closest Town:** Libby

4 KooKooSint Sheep Viewing Area

Description: This small meadow flanked by rocky outcroppings often provides opportunities to view bighorn sheep within 50 feet of your car—sometimes in herds of up to 100. Wildlife information signs are present at the site. The best time to view sheep is from March 1-May 31, and during the November 15-December 31 breeding season. Bighorns may be seen anywhere along Montana 200 for about seven miles on either side of this area. A few miles to the west on an island close to where the Clark Fork and Thompson Rivers join, look for elk in the spring and osprey, great blue herons, and waterfowl during the summer.

Directions: From Thompson Falls, drive 8 miles east on Montana 200.

Ownership: PVT, State of MT, USFS (826-3821)
Size: 1/4 acre **Closest Town:** Thompson Falls

5 | Smith Lake Waterfowl Production Area

Kalispell
Urban Site

Description: This large waterfowl area with extensive marshes and a significant lake is a good area for viewing shorebirds (phalaropes, yellowlegs, killdeer) and waterfowl (mallards, widgeons, pintails, gadwalls). Also look for nesting Canada geese, grebes, and assorted gulls. Other species of special interest include tundra swans in late March and early April, and American bitterns. In the spring and fall look for sandhill cranes in the western grassy meadows. Also look for bluebirds along the road on the way in. Smith Lake and Ashley Creek are open year-round to boating—a good way to view the varied wildlife. The upland areas are closed from March 1-July 1.

Directions: *From Kalispell, follow U.S. 2 west for seven miles to Big Horn Drive. Turn south on Big Horn Drive, then take Smith Lake Road to the Kila Fishing Access.*

Ownership: MDFWP, USFWS (755-4375)
Size: 1,040 acres   **Closest Town:** Kalispell

A young bighorn ram rubs the face of an older ram during a social visit. Bighorn sheep provide excellent opportunities for wildlife viewing at several sites, including KooKooSint near Thompson Falls. RALEIGH MEADE

6 | **Creston National Fish Hatchery**

Description: Situated along a beautiful spring creek, this hatchery raises both rainbow and cutthroat trout and produces eggs for propagation. At its peak, it holds over one million fish, with four to six million rainbow eggs produced annually. The raceways immediately adjacent to the buildings are open for public viewing. The building where spawning occurs has displays explaining how fish eggs are fertilized, how they develop, and how they hatch. Watch the spawning procedures between January and March. The hatchery's maximum fish populations are between April and June, but it always has one section with large numbers of eight- to ten-pound trout. Many fish-eating birds including osprey, great blue herons, kingfishers, and magpies can be seen in the vicinity. The pond and picnic area across the road from the hatchery almost always has several Canada geese broods in the summer. The hatchery is open daily from 7:30 a.m.-4 p.m.

Directions: From Big Fork, take Montana 35 north towards Creston and follow for about nine miles. Just east of Creston, take Creston Hatchery Road and drive about one mile to the hatchery.

Ownership: USFWS (755-7870)
Size: 74 acres **Closest Town:** Creston

7 | **Wild Horse Island**

Description: This largely undeveloped island in Flathead Lake with flower-covered uplands and forested slopes is the largest island in the largest freshwater lake west of Minnesota. Look in the high rocky area in the northwest corner for a herd of about 100 bighorn sheep. Also look for nesting bald eagles, waterfowl, osprey, goshawks, mule deer, coyotes, marmots, mink, numerous songbirds—and a few remaining wild horses. To preserve the island's natural features, there are no visitor facilities or public docks, so boats must be beached. There are 54 private lots on the island; please respect their rights. Hiking is possible on the numerous unofficial state land trails.

Directions: Take U.S. 93 to Polson. Island visitors can either take a tour boat from Polson, or rent a boat in Big Arm along the west side of the lake.

Ownership: MDFWP (752-5501)
Size: 2,165 acres **Closest Town:** Polson

8 | **Swan River National Wildlife Refuge**

Description: This undisturbed and undeveloped refuge contains extensive swampland and coniferous forest. The refuge is home to elk, deer, moose, grizzly bear, and black bear. Its 171 bird species include bald eagles, great blue herons, and black terns; a walk along Bog Road or a Swan River canoe trip are both excellent for birding. In the spring watch for tundra swans, nesting bald eagles, and Canada geese. In the summer look for wood ducks and yellowlegs. A canoe trip is the best way to see the refuge. Put in at the first county bridge upstream from Swan Lake off the Porcupine Road; it's an easy three- to four-mile float. To take-out, paddle across Swan Lake to a Forest Service boat ramp about 1 1/2 miles up the lake's northeastern shore. The southern shore is a good place to view a great blue heron rookery near the mouth of Spring Creek. Although the refuge is closed from March 1-July 1, floating on the river is still permitted.

Directions: *Take Montana 83 to the southern end of Swan Lake and look for the Swan River National Wildlife Refuge sign. A few hundred feet to the north of this sign is Bog Road. It's typically impassable and is more suited to foot traffic than vehicles.*

Ownership: USFWS (755-4375)
Size: 1,568 acres **Closest Town:** Swan Lake

Great blue herons are stately birds of marshes, lakeshores, and streams. They are commonly seen along waterways in western Montana, including the Swan River. RALEIGH MEADE

9 | **Old Squeezer Loop Road**

Description: This small creek-bottom area in a thick pine forest very near the mountains is an outstanding birding area. Both of the short loop trails (1/4 and 1/2 mile) have several benches for viewing and pass though grassy meadows, swamps, open hillsides, and timbered areas. Watch for Swainson's thrushes, redstarts, Vaux's swifts, hummingbirds, hairy woodpeckers, and warblers. May and June are usually the best months for birdwatching. White-tailed deer and elk frequent the area. Look for white-bog orchids in the wet areas along the road and trails.

Directions: Follow Montana 35 to the Swan River State Forest headquarters. Directly across from the headquarters, take Goat Creek Road (FS Road 554) east for 1.5 miles. At the fork in the road, go right on Old Squeezer Loop Road and follow for about two miles.

Ownership: DSL (754-2301)
Size: 1/2 mile **Closest Town:** Swan Lake   **P**

10 | **Ninepipe National Wildlife Refuge and State Wildlife Management Area**

Description: This exceptional wetland complex contains over 800 glacial potholes and a 1,770-acre reservoir. It's a terrific birding spot; more than 180 bird species have been recorded here. Look for waterfowl and colonial nesting birds including cormorants, great blue herons, and California and ring-billed gulls on islands on the west side of the main reservoir. One of the best viewing places is the picnic area; follow Secondary 212 for about two miles, and then take Ninepipe Road across the dike. Several small ponds also offer opportunities for close-up viewing and photography of waterfowl; turn west off U.S. 93 onto Duck Road, one mile north of its intersection with Secondary 212. Other birds include shorebirds, Canada geese, bald eagles, yellow-headed blackbirds, and pheasants. Area maps and bird lists are available at various entry points.

Directions: Four miles south of Ronan (45 miles north of Missoula), watch for refuge and WMA signs on U.S. 93 (Ninepipe is along the west side of the highway).

Ownership: MDFWP, USFWS (644-2211)
Size: 5,037 acres **Closest Town:** Ronan   **P**

 Bison were nearly eliminated from the United States in the late 1890s, but a small, wild herd survived in Yellowstone National Park. Today, both Yellowstone and the National Bison Range near Moiese contain substantial herds.

11 National Bison Range

Description: One of the oldest and most spectacular units in the entire national wildlife refuge system, this area contains steep, grassy hills and coniferous forests. The bison here number 300-500 animals, and are usually readily visible. Visitors may drive either a scenic two-hour loop (19 miles) or a shorter 1/2 hour loop (from late October to mid-May, the short loop is open but only a five-mile section of the longer loop is open). Along the drive, you can view bison, pronghorn, elk, bighorn sheep, white-tailed and mule deer, and occasionally mountain goats, making the range ideal for wildlife photography. Seasonal highlights include newborn bison calves in mid-April through May, blue grouse mating rituals in May (the Bitterroot Trail is a likely spot), elk bugling in September, and bighorn sheep anytime during the summer. Birdwatchers should look for Clark's nutcracker and Lewis' woodpecker as well as raptors and waterfowl. The visitor's center has excellent wildlife exhibits. It is open daily in the summer from 8 a.m.-8 p.m., and on weekdays only in the winter from 8 a.m-4:30 p.m. The refuge's visitor center, its nature trails, and even its environmental education program have been specially designed to meet the needs of people with disabilities.

Directions: From Ravalli, drive west on Montana 200 for six miles to Dixon, then north on Secondary 212 for four miles to the refuge entrance at Moiese.

Ownership: USFWS (644-2211)
Size: 18,541 acres **Closest Town:** Moiese   P ⛱ ▦ ♿ 🚶

Elk graze at the National Bison Range, one of western Montana's premier wildlife areas. Visitors are likely to see elk, bison, bighorn sheep, and pronghorn, along with smaller animals. MICHAEL S. SAMPLE.

12 | Clearwater Canoe Trail

Description: This truly exceptional, one- to two-hour easy canoe trip flows through a dense willow marsh on an isolated portion of the Clearwater River. There's an information board with maps at the put-in. It is an outstanding opportunity to view warblers, nesting common loons, bitterns, catbirds, snipe, great blue herons, belted kingfishers, and wood ducks. Turtles, large fish, muskrat, beaver, and dragonflies are common. It's a great trip for kids and adults alike. The last part of the trip crosses the top of Seeley Lake, so skirt the shore if the wind is strong. A 30-minute (approximate) return hiking trail winds by the river and wetlands and eliminates shuttle problems. Watch for white-tailed deer. Brochures about the canoe trail are available at the Seeley Lake Ranger Station.

Directions: From Seeley Lake, drive four miles north on Montana 83. Turn west at the Clearwater Canoe Trail sign and proceed a short distance to the put-in. The canoe take-out and start of the return trail are at the Seeley Lake Ranger Station, also a short distance from Montana 83.

Ownership: USFS (677-2233)
Size: Four-mile float, 1.5-mile return walk
Closest Town: Seeley Lake

P

13 | Clearwater Chain-of-Lakes Loon Driving Tour

Description: This highly scenic chain of lakes provides easily accessible viewing of red-necked grebes, waterfowl, and osprey, as well as the largest population of nesting common loons in the western United States. Look for nests on the small islands or marshy sections of the lakes, but do not approach closer than 200 feet as the loons may abandon their nests. Look across Salmon Lake to view muskrat houses and a beaver lodge. At Alva Lake look for northern harriers and nesting osprey. At Seeley Lake, painted turtles and leopard frogs are common. White-tailed deer are abundant along the route. A tour brochure is available from the USFS at the Seeley Lake Ranger Station just north of the town of Seeley Lake and from the Lolo National Forest office in Missoula.

Directions: From the junction of Montana 83 and Montana 200, drive north and stop at the designated points right off the road at Salmon, Seeley, Alva, and Rainy Lakes.

Ownership: USFS (677-2233)
Size: 18-mile drive
Closest Town: Seeley Lake

 Loons are symbols of wild country, and Montana has the largest population of nesting common loons west of the Mississippi. The Clearwater Chain-of-Lakes tour provides a good chance of viewing these diving birds.

14 Blackfoot-Clearwater WMA

Description: The diverse habitat of this area's rolling foothills and forests contains considerable birdlife, including pileated woodpeckers, Clark's nutcrackers, western and mountain bluebirds, and western tanagers. On the east side, look for waterfowl, sandhill cranes, and bald eagles near some woodland ponds and wetlands. Ring-necked ducks and three-toed woodpeckers have been seen here, and snow geese are sometimes spotted during migration. The area is closed to all entry from about November 30 to May 15, but large numbers of elk can be viewed from the Montana 83 turnout during the winter months. While there are no designated hiking trails, a number of roads can be driven or bicycled to view wildlife, and the open terrain lends itself to walking. Three miles northeast from the area, Upsata Lake is a predictable spot to see loons and waterfowl.

Directions: From Missoula, take Montana 200 east to Clearwater Junction (the junction of Montana 200 and Montana 83). Turn north on Montana 83 and follow for .3 mile to the viewing area. You can drive through the area by proceeding north on Montana 83 to the first road going right (east). It's a fair dirt road, about six miles long and suitable for most cars, that passes through the wildlife area. At the road's end, turn left and follow for three miles to Upsata Lake. A right turn here takes you to Montana 200.

Ownership: MDFWP (542-5523)
Size: 49,458 acres **Closest Town:** Seeley Lake   **P**

15 Kelly Island   *Missoula Urban Site*

Description: The habitat of this large, undeveloped island in the Clark Fork River is a unique mix of cottonwood bottoms, large meadows, and ponderosa pine forests with remarkable wildlife populations. Waterfowl concentrate in the winter and spring; the numerous backwater sloughs provide ideal resting spots. Around March the great blue herons begin to gather at the island's historic nesting area. Canada geese also nest on the island, sometimes in the heron nests. Wood duck boxes and goose-nesting platforms have been erected here. Red-tailed hawks, kestrels, and great horned owls also commonly nest on the island. This is a good spot to see Lewis' woodpeckers and bald eagles. White-tailed deer are extremely abundant and seen year-round, while beaver are common and foxes are seen occasionally. While river crossing can be difficult, once you're on the island it's easy to get around on a myriad of well-worn animal trails. When there's enough snow, Kelly Island is a unique place for cross-country skiing.

Directions: In Missoula, take Spurgin Road to the Fishing Access Site on the south side of Kelly Island, or take Mullan Road to the Kelly Island Fishing Access on the north side. You can either boat or wade across the river, but be careful to look for riffles; don't try wading if the water is high.

Ownership: MDFWP (542-5500)
Size: 631 acres **Closest Town:** Missoula   **P**

Although not quite ready to fly, a young great horned owl already displays the characteristics of a formidable hunter—keen eyes, sharp beak, and strong talons. Great horned owls are one of Montana's most common winged predators, sometimes even hunting during the day. MICHAEL S. SAMPLE

16 Rocky Mountain Elk Foundation Wildlife Visitor Center

Missoula Urban Site

Description: This visitor center features exceptional taxidermy of elk and other North American wildlife, including grizzly bears, mountain goats, bobcats, and mule deer. There are several world-record size elk mounts and several displays on elk and their habitat. The center displays some of the nation's best wildlife art, including a life-size bronze bull elk. The 50-seat theatre features videos about elk and other wildlife. The visitor center is open seven days a week; hours typically are 8:30 a.m-5:00 p.m. Monday through Friday and 11:00 a.m-4:00 p.m. on the weekends, but they are subject to change. The Rocky Mountain Elk Foundation is a non-profit organization dedicated to raising funds to benefit elk and their habitat.

Directions: In Missoula, 2291 West Broadway.

Ownership: PVT (1-800-843-7633)
Size: 2,000 sq. feet **Closest Town:** Missoula P

17 Greenough Park

Missoula Urban Site

Description: This outstanding city park runs along the clean and beautiful Rattlesnake Creek for about one mile and is a diverse mix of cottonwood bottomlands and coniferous forest. A paved trail runs the length of the park and numerous unpaved paths go near the creek and toward more undisturbed places. One of Missoula's top birding areas, more than 100 bird species have been identified here. In the spring and summer it's an especially good area to see warblers, vireos, orioles, black-headed grosbeaks, Lewis's woodpeckers, and calliope hummingbirds. In the winter look for pygmy owls, winter wrens, pine grosbeaks, barred owls, and hordes of Bohemian waxwings. Along the stream watch for dippers, belted kingfishers, and spotted sandpipers. Pileated woodpeckers are also frequently sighted, and white-tailed deer and an occasional black bear (early mornings in the fall) can be seen.

Directions: In Missoula, take Van Buren Avenue to Locust. Turn west on Locust until you hit Monroe Street, where you'll see a sign for Greenough Park.

Ownership: City of Missoula (721-7275)
Size: 42 acres **Closest Town:** Missoula P A 凸 & ☆

 In Montana forests, about one-fourth of the birds are cavity nesters, making their homes either in standing dead trees or within the heartwood of live trees.

| **18** | **Lee Metcalf National Wildlife Refuge** |

Description: This refuge is a diverse combination of wetlands and forested riverbottom habitat of the Bitterroot River. Most of the refuge is quite accessible and good for walking or viewing from your car. It's an exceptional place to watch nesting osprey; there are typically 20 nests or more on the refuge. In the spring look for Canada geese nesting in osprey nests, and in early April watch osprey reclaiming their nests. White-tailed deer are especially visible, as are tundra swans and other waterfowl during spring migration (March and April). Bald eagles are often seen both in winter and spring, and coyotes, red fox, muskrats, mink, and painted turtles are common. A two-mile loop trail (open July 15-September 15) accesses four ponds in the southeast corner of the refuge, where several blinds allow close-up observation and photography of waterfowl and shorebirds. Year-round walking access is limited to the Picnic Area (140 acres), which has two .9-mile hiking trails.

Directions: Take U.S. 93 to Stevensville, then turn east onto the East Side Hwy. and follow to Wildfowl Lane. Take this road for 1.5 miles until you see the refuge boundary signs (Wildfowl Lane winds through the southern part of the refuge).

Ownership: USFWS (777-5552)
Size: 2,800 acres **Closest Town:** Stevensville **P-⅄-🏠**

An adult osprey feeds a trio of young in their nest. At places such as the Lee Metcalf National Wildlife Refuge, nesting ospreys are frequently seen. HARRY ENGELS

19 | Skalkaho Game Preserve

Description: This isolated preserve is heavily forested with mountainous terrain and beautiful meadows. The area is totally closed to hunting. In the fall, view large concentrations of elk and hear them bugle, especially east of Fool Hen and Kneaves Lakes. You can see mountain goats around Dome Shaped Mountain near the junction of trail #313 and trail #86, which follow the ridge around Skalkaho Basin. Watch for moose along trail #321 in the Burnt Fork drainage. Mule deer, badgers, wolverines, coyotes, and black bear are common throughout the preserve. Mountain bicycling is a good way to see wildlife, especially during the fall road closure period Oct. 15 - Dec 1. Trail #313 offers some outstanding opportunities for overnight cross-country ski trips. Since only the first ten miles of Montana 38 are plowed, winter wildlife viewing would depend on the snow depth.

Directions: From Hamilton, travel three miles south on U.S. 93, then turn east on Montana 38 (Skalkaho Hwy.) and proceed 27 miles east to the top of the pass. Turn north on FS Road 1352 (closed to all motorized vehicles from October 15-December 1) and drive for five miles into the Skalkaho Basin (past Dam Lake).

Ownership: USFS (777-5461)
Size: 23,000 acres **Closest Town:** Hamilton

20 | Broad Axe Lodge and Restaurant

Description: This lodge and restaurant overlooks a scenic steep hillside with exceptional year-round bighorn sheep viewing. The restaurant provides binoculars upon request and the employees gladly show you where to look. Golden eagles frequently soar over the hill, elk and white-tailed deer are common in the winter, and nighthawks are often seen in the summer. Also in the summer, see large numbers of hummingbirds attracted by the feeders that surround the restaurant. Non-diners are welcome any time in the parking area. The restaurant is open year-round (dinner only), but just on weekends in the winter. Call ahead for hours and reservations. Restaurant dinner prices range from $8 to $15.

Directions: Take U.S. 93 south to Sula, then follow the road that parallels the East Fork of the Bitterroot River for 5.5 miles to the lodge and restaurant.

Ownership: PVT (821-3878)
Closest Town: Sula

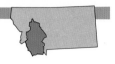

21 **Babcock Mountain Bighorn Sheep Viewing Area**
22 **Browns Lake**
23 **Sun River Canyon**
24 **Rocky Mountain Front Eagle Migration Area**
25 **Beartooth Wildlife Management Area**
26 **Gates of the Mountains**
27 **Spring Meadow Lake**
28 **Mount Helena**
29 **Canyon Ferry Wildlife Management Area**
30 **Lost Creek State Park**
31 **Mount Haggin Wildlife Management Area**
32 **Sheepshead Mountain Recreation Area**
33 **Lewis and Clark Caverns**
34 **Cattail Marsh Nature Trail**
35 **Big Sheep Creek**
36 **Red Rock Lakes**
   National Wildlife Refuge
37 **Cliff and Wade Lakes**

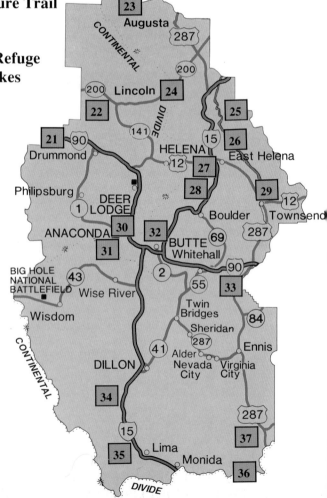

21 Babcock Mountain Bighorn Sheep Viewing Area

Description: This area has steep, grassy hillsides with rocky cliffs bordered by coniferous forest and is an excellent place to see bighorn sheep either from your car or while hiking. Hikers may choose either the Babcock Creek Trail, which follows the face of the sheep range for about a mile, or the Spring Creek Trail, which travels into the range. Both trails are closed during the bighorn lambing season (April through mid-May). The herd of about 150 animals is most visible in spring and winter. During spring lambing season, the ewes and lambs can usually be seen on the rocky cliffs. White-tailed deer are common, and golden eagles are frequently seen looking for pikas, golden-mantled ground squirrels, and snowshoe hares. The bitterroot, Montana's state flower, blooms in June on hot, dry sites. Rock Creek is a nationally famous trout stream noted for its water quality and beautiful scenery. In June, the creek experiences an amazing insect hatch of giant stoneflies (salmonflies), which lay their eggs and attract trout. Look carefully for moose at dawn near Rock Creek Road in the Spring Creek area, approximately three miles up Rock Creek on the east side of the road.

Directions: *From Missoula, drive 20 miles east on Interstate 90, exiting at Rock Creek. Travel south on Rock Creek Road for 4.5 miles and watch for an informational sign on bighorn sheep.*

Ownership: PVT, USFS (329-3814)
Size: 8,000 acres **Closest Town:** Clinton

22 Browns Lake

Description: Browns Lake is a shallow, productive 500-acre lake surrounded by open sagebrush grasslands and aspen groves. It's an extremely reliable place to see both bald eagles and osprey (especially in the spring), and almost always has significant numbers of waterfowl (divers as well as dabblers). The marsh in the lake's northeast corner is a reliable place to see see American coots, grebes, and herons and a likely spot to see avocets, yellow-headed blackbirds, and broods of Canada geese. Sandhill cranes, common loons, white pelicans, and upland sandpipers are often seen in the spring. Most birds are easily observed from a fair dirt road that goes around half the lake. Mountain bicycling and canoeing are good ways to see this area; the northeast corner of the lake, however, is closed to boating during the nesting season (April 1 - July 15). In good weather (this is a poor dirt road), continue north past Browns Lake for about two miles until you hit Montana 200. The area between the lake and the highway is a good place to see deer and sometimes elk. Hikers can visit the expansive Blackfoot Waterfowl Production Area (1,000 acres), which lies immediately adjacent to the east. Its small lakes and wetlands are visited infrequently. The numerous glacial potholes between Ovando and Browns Lake also provide exceptional birding.

Directions: *Take Montana 200 to Ovando, then follow the fishing access signs to Browns Lake.*

Ownership: PVT, USFWS, MDFWP (542-5500)
Size: 1,539 acres **Closest Town:** Ovando

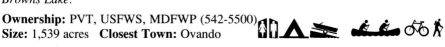

The Sun River area contains one of the largest native herds of bighorn sheep in North America.
MICHAEL S. SAMPLE

23 | Sun River Canyon

Description: At Sun River Canyon, the rolling prairies of the Northern Great Plains abruptly meet the rugged peaks of the Rockies, with steep cliffs and dramatic terrain. The area has exceptional wildlife diversity and abundance, with one of the largest herds of bighorn sheep in North America (800-1,000 animals). To see the sheep, either scan the area around the Home Gulch campground or walk in either Hannan Gulch or Wagner Basin. (The road to Hannan Gulch is about two miles up the canyon on the north side of the road. After the first half-mile it's a rugged four-wheel drive road that's better suited for walking or mountain bicycling. To reach Wagner Basin, take the Hannan Gulch Road across the Sun River, go 1/8 mile and turn right on a poorly maintained public dirt road. Follow the road for less than a half-mile past a few cabins until it ends near a steep cliff, and then follow the trail for about a mile into Wagner Basin. Cross-country skiing is possible when there's adequate snowfall.) Sun River Canyon is also a good area to see elk, deer, and raptors—especially eagles, which migrate in significant numbers along the edge of the mountains. In the summer, look for beavers, raptors, and songbirds near the river. In the winter and spring, the sheep are especially visible close to the road, which is well-maintained and well-plowed. Immediately southeast of the Sun River Canyon is the State of Montana's 20,000-acre Sun River Wildlife Management Area, which winters one of the state's largest elk populations. The WMA is closed to public access in the winter, but elk can be viewed from any of several nearby roads. In the summer, drive, hike, or mountain bicycle in the WMA to see tundra swans, Canada geese, herons, and sometimes white pelicans on numerous small lakes and sharp-tailed grouse, coyotes, and long-billed curlews on the grassy uplands.

Directions: At Augusta, turn northwest off U.S. 287 onto Sun River Road. Follow this road for four miles, turning right at the fork in the road. Proceed northwest for about 15 miles to Sun River Canyon.

Ownership: USFS (466-5341)
Size: 4,000 acres **Closest Town**: Augusta

Winter-killed elk and other ungulates are an important food source for grizzly bears, especially along the Rocky Mountain Front. MICHAEL S. SAMPLE

24 | Rocky Mountain Front Eagle Migration Area

Description: This scenic mountain area is part of a major migration route for eagles (primarily golden but some bald) along the east front of the Rocky Mountains, where in March the strong westerly winds rushing over the foothills create the lift eagles need for migration. In fact, this area is where the most migrating golden eagles have ever been observed in the United States in a single day. During key migration times, eagles can sometimes be seen in large numbers from a distance of 100-500 feet. The best springtime eagle-watching is in March (as many as 818 golden eagles and 129 bald eagles have been seen between March 12 and April 3), but migration continues through May. For the fall migration, mid-September through October is best. The best afternoon viewing sites are from highway pullouts about 1/4 mile west of the Dearborn River. In the morning the flight tends to be further out on the plains. Other raptors one might see include red-tailed hawks, rough-legged hawks, sharp-shinned hawks, and northern goshawks. Waterfowl are also sighted occasionally; look for snow geese, tundra swans, and Canada geese.

Directions: From Lincoln, drive east on Montana 200 for 15 miles to the top of Rogers Pass. The best place to view the eagles is between the mouth of the canyon east of the pass and Bowman's Corners, which is at the junction of Montana 200 and U.S. 287.

Ownership: USFS (362-4265)
Closest Town: Lincoln

P

25 | Beartooth Wildlife Management Area

Description: The beautiful grass and sagebrush hills of this WMA gradually give way to forested uplands with rugged rocky outcroppings. It's notable for its large populations of elk and bighorn sheep, as well as an interesting prairie dog town. The WMA is easily accessible via fair dirt roads, where wildlife can be viewed from your car. You can hike up one of the roads that follows a creek (Cottonwood, Elkhorn, and Willow are good bets), some of which are closed to vehicle use (Cottonwood year-round and Elkhorn from May 15 - August 31) but open to mountain bicycling. If you're hiking, go up one of the creek bottoms and then follow one of the ridgelines back down. The birding is always good along the creeks (especially along Cottonwood Creek downstream to the lake), and the ridge hikes often lead to bighorn sheep, deer, and elk. Look for the prairie dog town on the north side of the road not long after you reach the WMA (there's an informational sign). On the way past Holter Lake, look for waterfowl, white pelicans, common loons, and peregrine falcons. The WMA is closed to public use from December 1 - May 14.

Directions: From Helena, take Interstate 15 north to Wolf Creek. Turn north on Missouri River Road until you reach the Holter Lake access road. Follow this road along the east shore of Holter Lake for about six miles to the Beartooth WMA.

Ownership: MDFWP (454-3441)
Size: 31,798 acres
Closest Town: Wolf Creek

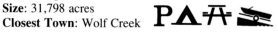

| 26 | **Gates of the Mountains** |

Description: This is an approximately two-hour boat tour along one of the most scenic sections of the Missouri River. The trip often provides close-up views of bighorn sheep, mountain goats, and mule deer. Also look for bald eagles, osprey, red-tailed hawks, turkey vultures, great horned owls, and peregrine falcons. Frequently seen waterfowl are mergansers, mallards, white pelicans, and common loons (in the spring and fall only). Before its return, the boat tour stops at the Meriweather Picnic Area, from which three hiking trails offer additional wildlife viewing opportunites. Depending on the boat schedule, hikers can usually catch a later boat back. Tour fares range between $2.50 - $5.50, depending upon age.

Directions: From Helena, drive 20 miles north on Interstate 15 and take the Gates of the Mountains exit. Proceed 2.8 miles to the Gates of the Mountains boat tour. There is a public boat launch here ($3 per boat on a trailer, and $2 per boat on a car rack) in addition to the private boat tours.

Ownership: PVT (458-5241)
Size: 12 miles roundtrip
Closest Town: Helena

| 27 | **Spring Meadow Lake** | *Helena Urban Site* |

Description: This park is a crystalline spring-fed lake surrounded by willows and cottonwoods. Nearby uplands with sagebrush and rabbitbrush add to the diverse birdlife. Spring Meadow is a solid birdwatching spot during migration times, and the lake often has Canada geese, American coots, mallards, and occasionally common loons. The willows and cottonwoods harbor warblers, vireos, and other songbirds. This dense lakeside vegetation also houses rabbits, muskrats, and skunks. On summer evenings one can sometimes see bats or nighthawks. Five kinds of snakes have been reported from the area, and the clear waters are alive with painted turtles, trout, largemouth bass, and perch. Heavy swimming use at the north end of the lake can reduce wildlife viewing opportunities in the summer. But early in the morning, or at other times of year, it affords good wildlife watching very close to town. There's a one-mile nature trail around the lake with wildlife information signs; brochures are available at the park entrance.

Direction: From Helena, follow U.S. 12 west toward Missoula. Before you leave town, turn right (north) on Joslyn Street, then curve left onto Country Club Avenue and follow the sign to Spring Meadow Lake.

Ownership: MDFWP (444-2535)
Size: 56 acres **Closest Town**: Helena

| 28 | **Mount Helena** | *Helena Urban Site* |

Description: Mt. Helena is a large, wild city park that adjoins nearly 11,000 acres of undeveloped national forest land. A variety of wildlife inhabits its scattered Douglas-fir forests and expansive grassland areas. Two well marked trails leave the parking area and encircle the mountain, climbing 1,200 feet to Mt. Helena's mile-high summit. For the best wildlife viewing on a short walk, follow trail #1906 as it leaves the parking area to the west. After about 200 yards turn right on the Prairie Trail at the first marked trail junction. Prairie Trail gently climbs for two miles through open grasslands below the towering limestone intersection with the Westside Trail. The expansive view along the edge of the cliffs and forests provide opportunities to see prairie falcons, mountain bluebirds, meadowlarks, rufous-sided towhees, rock wrens, juncos, and magpies. White-tailed deer are common, and an occasional black bear, red fox, or coyote may be seen. For a longer hike, follow Westside Trail to the Mt. Helena Ridge National Recreation Trail, which offers seven more miles of open ridge walking through the Helena National Forest to the old Park City townsite.

Directions: In Helena, follow Adams Street west until you reach the parking area.

Ownership: City of Helena (442-9920)
Size: 620 acres **Closest Town:** Helena

| 29 | **Canyon Ferry Wildlife Management Area** |

Description: This exceptional wetland and river bottom area where the Missouri River enters Canyon Ferry Reservoir is a good place to see migrating waterfowl (pintails and tundra swans in March) and many nesting birds, including Canada geese, double-crested cormorants, American avocets, and osprey. Common loons are frequently seen in large numbers during spring and fall migration. Commonly seen mammals include white-tailed deer and beaver, while river otter are seen infrequently. The best place to see mammals is in the delta portion of the WMA. This area can be reached via numerous gravel roads off the east side of U.S. 287. The best place to view waterfowl and shorebirds is Pond Three on the east side of the WMA. To get to the pond, take U.S. 12 east from Townsend and turn left (north) onto Harrison Road, which turns into Canton Road. The road will deadend at a parking area near the south end of Pond Three. A map of the WMA is available from the USFS and MDFWP offices in Townsend. Between November and mid-December a large number of bald eagles—as many as 200—typically congregate at the opposite end of Canyon Ferry Reservoir below Canyon Ferry dam to feed on spawning kokanee salmon.

Directions: The WMA begins one mile north of Townsend and continues for two miles along the east side of U.S. 287. It can be reached by gravel roads that turn off of U.S. 287. Or, from Townsend, follow U.S. 12 east for a short distance, then turn north onto Harrison Road.

Ownership: BuRec., Managed by MDFWP (266-3367)
Size: 5,000 acres **Closest Town:** Townsend

30 | Lost Creek State Park

Description: This small state park is a narrow canyon with 1,200+ foot high limestone cliffs and a small stream with a beautiful falls. The rocky cliffs provide a home for bighorn sheep as well as easily observable mountain goats. One of the best places to see the goats is from a pullout (marked with informational signs) at the park entrance. The best time to see the sheep is during the winter and spring in the dry, open grasslands and scattered timber near the park entrance. While the sheep aren't usually as visible during summer and fall, they can often be seen in the Olsen Gulch area (about four miles to the west). Moose are frequently seen in the creekbottom area year-round, and mule deer are often sighted on the rocky hillsides. Look for black bears on the open hillsides in the spring. The short walk to Lost Creek Falls is the only established hiking trail, but hikers can scramble up the steep hillsides. For a longer walk, follow the old road (now closed to motorized vehicles) near the park road end, which goes west for about six miles before connecting to Foster Creek. Look for moose in the creek bottom and mule deer on the hillsides. The two-mile park road is excellent for cross-country skiing and viewing winter wildlife.

Directions: From Interstate 90, take Montana 1 to Anaconda. Approximately two miles east of Anaconda take Galen Road, following signs to the park.

Ownership: USFS, MDFWP (542-5500)
Size: 500 acres
Closest Town: Anaconda

A pair of Canada geese lead their goslings on a quiet stretch of water. Canada geese nest along many rivers and lakes in Montana, including the Missouri River and Canyon Ferry Reservoir. MICHAEL S. SAMPLE

31 | **Mount Haggin Wildlife Management Area**

Description: Montana's largest WMA, Mount Haggin is a stunning mix of aspen-dotted rolling hills, lush willow bottoms, and forested mountains, with the Pintlar Range looming in the background. It's a great place to see moose, elk, and nesting sandhill cranes. Its exceptional habitat diversity makes for good birdwatching—look for warblers, vireos, and thrushes in the bottomlands and raptors and grouse in the uplands. Good viewing spots include Dry Creek Road (Forest Road 2483), about one mile north of the vista area, and Home Ranch Road, about four miles south of the vista area. Home Ranch Road is frequently impassable, so hiking or mountain bicycling is recommended. Another good viewing area is a large meadow only a half-mile up the road from the turnoff to Home Ranch. There are no established hiking trails, but there are many unmarked trails. You are allowed to walk anywhere, and mountain bicycling has outstanding potential here. Mount Haggin is open to cross-country skiing in the winter, when the moose are particularly visible.

Directions: From Anaconda, take Montana 1 east for three miles until you reach Secondary 274. Heading south toward Wisdom, County 274 bisects the WMA near the Continental Divide. Look for Mule Ranch Vista area about 14 miles from Montana 1. There are informational signs on the west side of the road.

Ownership: MDFWP (994-4042)
Size: 54,137 acres **Closest Town:** Anaconda   P

32 | **Sheepshead Mountain Recreation Area** | *Butte Urban Site*

Description: This area is a mixture of meadows and marsh surrounded by thick forests, with several streams and a small lake. The area is totally accessible to persons with disabilities—campgrounds, day-use area, trails, bathrooms, and even a fishing area. It's a good place to see deer and occasionally a moose or elk. Waterfowl use the lake, especially during migration, and the paths along the small creek are usually alive with birds. Birds commonly seen are spotted sandpipers, killdeer, mountain bluebirds, nuthatches, and hairy and downy woodpeckers. The area is also home to pine squirrels, chipmunks, rabbits, badger, and porcupine. The facility is open from late May - September. Just south of Sheepshead, the 16-mile long Hail Columbia Gulch Road from Sheepshead to Rocker is a fair gravel road that's good for wildlife viewing. Near the junction of the Hail Columbia Gulch Road and the main road, look for warblers, vireos, and other birds in the thick streamside vegetation. Another few miles down the road, near the Lowland Campground, look for moose. Raptors are frequently seen in the meadows near the road.

Directions: From Butte, drive north on Interstate 15, exiting at Elk Park (mile post 138). Proceed west, following the signs to Sheepshead.

Ownership: USFS (494-2147)
Size: 156 acres **Closest Town**: Butte   P

| 33 | **Lewis and Clark Caverns** |

Description: This state park's beautiful limestone caverns are home to the only known maternity colony of western big-eared bats in Montana. Guided tours through the caverns take about two hours and are offered from May 1 - September 30. The bats are usually pointed out by the tour guide. A self-guided nature trail to the caverns explains the natural surroundings and is a good place to see a variety of birds, including rock and house wrens, mountain bluebirds, white-throated swifts, lazuli buntings, rufous hummingbirds, and both green-tailed and rufous-sided towhees. Prairie rattlesnakes, bullsnakes, and racers can be found near the caverns and along the trail. On the drive to the caverns, look for raptors (especially golden eagles and red-tailed hawks) overhead along the Jefferson River. Deer are common on the scenic three-mile drive to the visitor's center.

Directions: *From Three Forks, drive 19 miles west on Montana 2.*

Ownership: MDFWP (287-3541)
Size: 2,735 acres **Closest Town**: Three Forks

P△⚌⌂🏠$⦿ 🚶

Montana's Lewis and Clark Caverns is one of the best places to view western big-eared bats.
KRISTI DUBOIS

| 34 | **Cattail Marsh Nature Trail** |

Description: This is a small, easily accessible cattail marsh surrounded by dry uplands at the north end of Clark Canyon Reservoir. It's near the Interstate, yet one can get close-up views of waterfowl, blackbirds (yellow-headed as well as red-wing), rails, American coots, and common snipe. Look for cliff swallows and their mud nests on the rocky cliffs, yellow-bellied marmots near the rocks, antelope on the dry uplands, and trout near the large spring on the west side of the trail. Wildlife information signs are present. There's also great shorebird and waterfowl viewing about five miles from the cattail marsh area at the extensive mudflats near the south end of Clark Canyon Reservoir. Take the Red Rock exit off Interstate 15 and head north about 2.5 miles until you reach a cattleguard. From there, continue north toward the reservoir shore rather than following the main gravel road that turns west.

Directions: From Dillon, drive south on Interstate 15 and take exit 44 at Clark Canyon (Secondary 324). Follow the road over the dam and take the first right at the river fishing access sign. The handicapped-accessible trail is on an old paved road immediately below the dam.

Ownership: BuRec (683-6472)
Size: 30 acres **Closest Town:** Dillon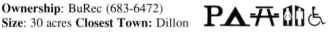

| 35 | **Big Sheep Creek** |

Description: This isolated, spectacular mountain valley is a narrow canyon with a good dirt road that often provides exceptional opportunities to view bighorn sheep near your vehicle. Even though it's not far from the Interstate, it's a good spot to see raptors (especially golden eagles), mule deer, antelope, and sometimes elk. It also has great wildflowers in the early summer. The best place to view sheep is about 4.5 miles up the road where the canyon gets narrow and rocky. Hikers might also try the Hidden Pasture Trail (about four miles up the road) that heads south from Big Sheep Creek Road through open country with great views. On Muddy Creek Road (about six miles from the frontage road), look for elk, deer, and mountain cottontail rabbits. This is also a reliable place to see pygmy rabbits, found only in the southwestern corner of Montana. There's a significant sage grouse population in the upper Big Sheep Creek area. One of the larger strutting grounds is about 20 miles from the frontage road, where Alkali Creek crosses the road in Section Two. The best viewing is during mid- to late-April at morning's first light.

Directions: Take Interstate 15 to Dell, then proceed south on the frontage road for 1.5 miles. Turn right onto Big Sheep Creek Road and follow it for about 4.5 miles.

Ownership: BLM (683-2337)
Size: 12,000+ acres **Closest Town:** Dell   **Pᐃᎆ🏕**

36 | **Red Rock Lakes National Wildlife Refuge**

Description: This large and extremely remote refuge contains nearly 13,000 acres of wetlands and peaks that rise sharply to over 9,000 feet. It's been called the most beautiful national wildlife refuge in the United States. The trumpeter swan was brought back from near-extinction here; about 300-500 swans live and breed on the refuge, the largest breeding population in the lower United States. The best place to view swans is from the Upper Lake Campground and the Lower Lake turnout; Shambow Pond and Culver Pond are also good. More than 50,000 ducks and geese may be present at migration times. Shorebirds such as long-billed curlews, willets, and American avocets frequent the mud flats near the marshes, while gulls, terns, and white pelicans are often viewed winging over the water. Look for moose in the willows near Upper Lake campground and along the south shore of Upper Lake. Look for sandhill cranes west of Lower Red Rock Lake and in the uplands south of Upper Red Rock Lake. The Centennial Valley has a notable concentration of raptors, especially red-tailed hawks, ferruginous hawks, Swainson's hawks, and peregrine falcons. Other species often seen include pronghorn antelope, deer, and elk. Much of the refuge can be seen from the car when the weather's good. An exceptional day-long canoe trip between the upper and lower lakes (check with refuge headquarters for water levels and directions) is open from September 15 until freeze-up. There's also good hiking along Odell or Red Rock Creeks, and great mountain bicycling on numerous unimproved roads. Check at Refuge headquarters at Lakeview for additional information.

Directions *From Monida (immediately off Interstate 15) turn east on a gravel road, traveling 28 miles to the refuge entrance. If you are coming from West Yellowstone, follow U.S. 20 for about 12 miles west to the junction with Montana 87. Proceed north on Montana 87 for five miles and turn west onto Red Rock Pass Road, following for about 20 miles to the refuge entrance.*

Ownership: USFWS
Size: 42,525 acres **Closest Town:** Monida

The Centennial Mountains on the Montana—Idaho border tower above Red Rock Lakes National Wildlife Refuge, often called the most beautiful national wildlife refuge in the United States. MICHAEL S. SAMPLE

37 | Cliff and Wade Lakes

Description: These two unique lakes sit on a geologic fault, forming a chasm with cliffs surrounding much of the lakes. Cliff Lake is the larger of the two and is more isolated. Wade Lake is more accessible and more used; it's spring-fed and stays partly ice-free in the winter. Both lakes support many nesting raptors; look for prairie falcons, bald eagles, and osprey (don't disturb or approach nesting raptors). Waterfowl and beaver are common on both lakes. In the winter, Wade Lake is a good place to see river otters and occasionally, trumpeter swans. Larger mammals frequently seen include deer, elk, and moose, which are even more numerous and visible in the winter. Cliff Lake offers some exceptional canoeing, especially in the remote coves (canoes can be rented at the Wade Lake Resort). A hiking trail above Cliff Lake goes to the Forest Service's Cliff Lake Natural Area. This area also can be a great place for cross-country skiing to see moose and elk in the winter. For overnight accommodations contact Wade Lake Resort, 682-7560.

Direction: *Just north of the junction of U.S. 287 and Montana 87, take Forest Road 8381. Follow this fair gravel road for about six miles to the lakes (look for signs).*

Ownership: USFS (682-4253)
Size: 890 acres
Closest Town: Ennis

Moose are found over much of western Montana, including Cliff and Wade lakes. Moose are the largest member of the deer family. MICHAEL S. SAMPLE

| 38 | **Our Lake** |

Description: One of the few alpine lakes along the Rocky Mountain Front, Our Lake is a dependable place to see mountain goats. From the saddle that overlooks the lake, one gets an outstanding panorama of the Bob Marshall Wilderness, including the Chinese Wall. On the hike in look for bluebirds and three-toed woodpeckers in a recent burn area. Mountain goats can usually be spotted near the lake or on the nearby cliffs. Pikas and marmots are common about the rocky scree. Yellowstone cutthroat trout are often visible in the very clear lake. Grizzly bears, mule deer, coyotes, grouse, pine marten, and eagles are all area residents. Wildflowers are abundant. The lake is used heavily on weekends. It's normally accessible from June-October, but July and August are the only sure access times.

Directions: From Choteau, drive north on U.S. 89 for five miles. Turn west on County Road 144 (Teton Road) and follow it for 15 miles. At the Ear Mountain Ranger Station sign, turn south on County Road 109 (South Fork Teton Road) and drive nine miles to the end of the road. Hike along FS Trail 184 for 3.5 miles to Our Lake.

Ownership: USFS (466-5341)
Size: 700 acres **Closest Town:** Choteau **P**

| 39 | **Pine Butte Swamp Preserve** |

Description: This unique private preserve is the largest wetland complex along the Rocky Mountain Front and the grizzly bear's last stronghold on the plains. Its diverse habitats include wetlands, mountains, foothills, and prairie grasslands, with a sandstone butte looming 500 feet above the prairie and encircled on the north and west by a dense swamp. This swamp provides important habitat for the grizzly bear (the chances of actually seeing a bear are very remote) and more than 43 other mammals including beaver, muskrat, deer, and elk. The area's rich birdlife (more than 150 species have been recorded) ranges from warblers and vireos to long-billed curlews, sandhill cranes, and upland sandpipers. Sharp-tailed grouse are common, especially on several dancing grounds in the spring. Access to the preserve is limited to protect natural features. Contact the preserve manager (466-5526) for permission to walk in the swamp or on the butte. A nice walk not requiring permission starts across the road from the information signs, and a climb to the ridge offers a good view of the butte and surrounding swamp. From May through September, weekly stays with guided tours of the preserve are available at the Pine Butte Guest Ranch (466-2158).

Directions: From Choteau, drive north on U.S. 89 for five miles. Turn west on Teton Canyon Road and follow for 15 miles, then turn south, cross the Teton River, and proceed straight ahead for 3.5 miles until you reach an information sign.

Ownership: The Nature Conservancy (466-5526) **P**
Size: 18,000 acres **Closest Town:** Choteau

| 40 | **Blackleaf Wildlife Management Area** |

Description: This WMA abutting the Rocky Mountain Front contains many scenic habitats including limber pine on glacial outwash areas, rolling grasslands, and wet marshes. Outstanding wildflower displays can be seen in the spring and early summer. Probably the best place to view wildlife is Antelope Butte, a sandstone escarpment that escaped the glaciers. Grizzly and black bears frequent the area (parts of the WMA are closed each spring until July 1 due to grizzly use), as do mule deer and elk. At the south end of the butte are marshes and ponds with willows and aspen—good places to walk and look for waterfowl, shorebirds, and numerous songbirds. There are a large variety of raptors throughout the area: marsh hawks, golden eagles, merlins, and prairie falcons. Marmots and ground squirrels provide a solid prey base both for the raptors and for coyotes. Look for sharp-tailed grouse dancing grounds in the spring. The best time to see elk is in the winter, although from December 1-May 15 off-road travel is prohibited to minimize disturbances to wintering elk. However, the road is plowed to the east end of the WMA, where you can then proceed by car, foot, or skis, depending on the snow level. A herd of about 75 mountain goats can be seen year-round where the road deadends in stunningly beautiful Blackleaf Canyon. Park and walk west for less than a mile to where the canyon narrows. On the hike in, look for whitewash areas on the canyon walls in order to spot nesting raptors.

Directions: Take U.S. 89 to Bynum, and then drive west on Blackleaf Road for about 16 miles to the WMA.

Ownership: MDFWP (278-7754)
Size: 19,430 acres **Closest Town:** Bynum

Sharp-tailed grouse perform elaborate mating displays on communal grounds called "leks," returning to the same site each year. These spring rituals can be observed at Pine Butte Swamp Preserve and Blackleaf Wildlife Management Area.
MICHAEL S. SAMPLE

41 Freezeout Lake Wildlife Mangement Area

Description: Freezeout Lake is a large wetland complex that often has the largest waterfowl concentrations in Montana—up to a million birds during migration peaks (March-May, September-November). As many as 300,000 snow geese and 10,000 tundra swans have been observed at one time here. The third week in March and the first week in November are typically the peak dates for tundra swan migrations; the first week in April and the first week in November for snow geese. The spring migration numbers are usually larger and the birds are typically more approachable. Freezeout is also noted for its shorebird concentration. Other birds of special interest include long-billed curlews, white-faced ibis, black-crowned night herons, sandhill cranes, and black-necked stilts. Thousands of California, ring-billed, and Franklin's gulls have been banded at the refuge, with returns from as far away as Peru. During winter the most visible bird species include pheasants, sharp-tailed grouse, gray partridges, bald and golden eagles, rough-legged hawks, the rare gyrfalcon, great horned owls, and occasionally a snowy owl. Coyotes, foxes, jackrabbits, and long-tailed weasels also may be seen. This WMA has very good access—the only closures are during the waterfowl hunting season (October-December) to provide a waterfowl refuge. Hiking and canoeing are possible anywhere outside the closure. The headquarters office immediately off U.S. 89 has maps delineating the closed area, as well as refuge bird lists. Boating can be difficult in this shallow lake depending on water levels. The most popular driving route is the road around Pond 5, which is closed during the hunting season.

Directions: *From Choteau, drive ten miles south on U.S. 89.*

Ownership: MDFWP (467-2646)
Size: 11,350 acres **Closest Town:** Fairfield

The long-billed curlew is a large shorebird with a long, down-curved bill. It is frequently seen near open fields and grasslands both east and west of the mountains.
MICHAEL S. SAMPLE

| 42 | **Giant Springs State Park** | *Great Falls Urban Site* |

Description: This exceptional urban wildlife site contains the largest freshwater spring in the United States, discharging nearly 400 million gallons of water per day into the Missouri River. It's a great place to see trout, but the adjacent hatchery is even better. The Giant Springs fish hatchery has an excellent self-guided tour and a large outdoor show pond where you can feed eight- to twelve-pound rainbow trout. The Missouri River section that flows past Giant Springs is shallow, swift, and one of the last to freeze, so it attracts extraordinary concentrations of waterfowl in the winter. In the summer, ducks, Canada geese, white pelicans, and shorebirds are present. It's a top-notch birding site (over 150 species have been seen here), especially along the short trail that runs west from the springs. Look for bald eagles, common loons, and dippers in the winter, and prairie falcons, gray partridges, pheasants, gulls, and double-crested cormorants in the spring through fall. The visitor center (right across the roadway from the spring) features taxidermic mounts of grizzly and black bears, educational features on fish and bird recognition, wildlife photographs, and a mini-theatre that shows wildlife videos. It's open 8 a.m-5 p.m. Monday through Friday (8 a.m. to 7 p.m. weekdays and 10 a.m.-7 p.m. weekends in the summer).

Directions: From Great Falls, take River Road and turn north onto Giant Springs Road.

Ownership: MDFWP (454-3441)
Size: 117 acres **Closest Town:** Great Falls

Giant Springs State Park provides excellent viewing of rainbow trout, both in the hatchery raceways and in the spring itself. CRAIG & LIZ LARCOM

53

| 43 | **Benton Lake National Wildlife Refuge** |

Description: This easily accessible refuge—a rich, shallow prairie marsh surrounded by intensive agriculture—is one of the most productive waterfowl refuges in the United States, and one of the best places to see and photograph broods of ducks and geese. It is an important stop for migrating waterfowl during March-April and September-October, attracting ducks (up to 100,000), tundra swans (up to 4,500), snow geese (up to 40,000), and Canada geese (up to 1,000), as well as nearly 200 other bird species. It's a significant area for migrating shorebirds—one of only two places in Montana nominated to be part of an International Shorebird Reserve. Burrowing and short-eared owls also can be found here. Deer and pronghorn antelope are common, as are jackrabbits and long-tailed weasels in the winter. A drive along the nine-mile-long Prairie Marsh Wildlife Drive is the best way to view the refuge. It's open March 1-November 30, but the road may be closed during wet weather. This winding gravel road has numbered signs corresponding to an interpretive brochure available at the main information sign. Hiking and canoeing are also possible, but check at the refuge headquarters to find out which areas are open.

Directions: Just north of Great Falls, turn off U.S. 87 onto Bootlegger Trail (Secondary 225) and follow it approximately 12 miles to the refuge entrance on the left side of the road. From the turnoff, it's about 1.5 miles to the informational signs.

Ownership: USFWS (727-7400)
Size: 12,383 acres **Closest Town:** Great Falls

Thousands of snow geese fill the air at Benton Lake National Wildlife Refuge. Spectacular flights of snow geese also may be observed at Freezeout Lake. KRISTI DUBOIS

44 | Missouri River Recreation Road

Description: This 35-mile, slow-paced driving alternative to Interstate 15 follows the Missouri River through rocky canyons and rolling prairie. You often can see white pelicans, great blue herons, Canada geese, nesting wood ducks, and bald eagles, which are especially numerous in the winter. Look for a golden eagle nest at Eagle Rock, about six miles downstream from Craig. Other more frequently seen bird species include gulls (the black-headed ones are probably Franklin's gull), ducks, magpies, and bluebirds (look for bluebird houses on the fence posts). Deer and coyote are common, and beaver dams can be seen near the road on Little Prickly Pear Creek. The recreational road officially ends at Hardy Creek, but you can continue north on the frontage road through Cascade and on to Ulm, which is a good area for watching raptors in the spring.

Directions: The recreation road runs between Helena and Great Falls. From the south, take Interstate 15 exit 219 at Little Spring; from the north, take exit 247 at Hardy Creek.

Ownership: PVT, MDFWP (454-3441)
Size: 35 miles **Closest Town:** Cascade

45 | Rookery Wildlife Management Area
Havre
Urban Site

Description: This easily accessible site encompassing about four miles of the Milk River is an outstanding riverbottom area with mature cottonwoods, thick streamside vegetation, and some rugged and beautiful badlands country on the north side of the road. Its diverse habitats attract many bird species: American avocets, yellowlegs, great blue herons, pheasants, golden eagles, brown thrashers, Canada geese, mallards, and pintails. Several raptors nest near the river, including kestrels, great horned owls, and red-tailed hawks. White-tailed and mule deer are common. The best way to see the area is by walking on one of the many unmarked riverside paths, or by canoeing the Milk River. There are boat launch sites at the west and east ends of the WMA, providing access to an easy five-mile float trip. There is a small but dangerous weir several miles downriver, so do not extend your float. Off-road vehicles are prohibited.

Directions: From Havre, follow Seventh Ave. north (Secondary 232), crossing the railroad tracks and Milk River. Turn left on River Road and follow for about five miles to the WMA.

Ownership: MDFWP (228-9347)
Size: 2,276 acres **Closest Town:** Havre

46 **BR-12**

Description: This 200-acre prairie marsh in the midst of open grasslands is narrow and long—nearly a mile in length—making for a pleasant walk. It's a great place to view ducks, Canada geese, golden eagles, ferruginous hawks, Swainson's hawks, shorebirds, and songbirds for much of the year. In the spring, look for goldeneyes, redheads, canvasbacks, and ring-necked ducks in the thick cattail marsh at the north end, where there are also nesting structures for mallards. In the summer, broods of waterfowl are always present. Look for nesting waterfowl on the small islands. Muskrats, raccoons, and jackrabbits can be seen near the marsh, and pronghorn antelope are common. Look for mule deer in the woody draw below the dam. BR-12 is a relatively remote site, with no restrictions on access.

Directions: Take U.S. 2 to Zurich and drive one-half mile west of town to Zurich County Road. Turn north and travel nine miles to an unimproved dirt road on the east. You can either walk or drive a high-clearance vehicle on the road a short distance to reach the reservoir.

Ownership: BLM (265-5891)
Size: 1,800 acres **Closest Town:** Zurich

47 **Black Coulee National Wildlife Refuge**

Description: Black Coulee is a remote, substantial prairie marsh (much more so in wet years) surrounded by grass and sagebrush-covered draws and coulees. It's a good area for waterfowl (especially Canada geese and pintails), mule deer, golden eagles, and pronghorns. Tundra swans are often present during late October. Upland birds—sharp-tailed grouse and gray partridges—inhabit the drier areas. Access to the refuge is primarily by foot; the gate near the refuge sign is locked. It's a good hike to walk completely around the wetland.

Directions: From Turner, drive south on Secondary 241 for seven miles. Look for a gravel road and drive south for three miles, then east for one mile, and south again for .5 mile until you see the refuge sign on the left.

Ownership: PVT, USFWS (654-2863)
Size: 1,494 acres **Closest Town:** Turner

 The largest bird of prey in Montana is the golden eagle. Its wingspan can be as large as seven feet, and it can weigh up to thirteen pounds.

48 **Beaver Creek County Park**   *Havre*
Urban Site

Description: This 10,000-acre wild area is one of the largest county parks in the United States. It's a long, narrow corridor (about 17 miles long and about one mile wide) along the north slopes of the Bear Paw Mountains with a good paved road that passes through rolling grasslands, ponderosa pine forests, and aspen and cottonwood groves. Rocky cliffs and small ponds and lakes add to the scenic diversity. Birdwatchers can see warblers, vireos, rails, prairie falcons, and pheasants, as well as species of special interest such as the yellow-breasted chat and lazuli bunting along the creek. Watch for eagles just north of Daryl Marden Memorial on the scraggy butte. White-tailed and mule deer, elk, and bobcats also use the park, and coyotes and raccoons are plentiful. There are some springs in the park that provide open water for waterfowl in the winter; beaver dams are abundant near this area. Beaver Creek is open in the winter to snowmobiles and cross-country skiing. Further information is available at the Park Office at Camp Kiwanis, about ten miles into the park, where you also can pay the $5 user fee.

Directions: In Havre, follow 5th Avenue to Beaver Creek Road and drive nine miles to Beaver Creek County Park.

Ownership: Hill County (395-4565)
Size: 10,000 acres **Closest Town:** Havre

Mule deer are the most common deer in Montana. They are found in virtually all habitats. In many parts of Charlie Russell Country, mule deer may be seen in agricultural areas, especially at dawn and dusk. MICHAEL S. SAMPLE

| 49 | Upper Missouri National Wild and Scenic River |

Description: This 149-mile section is the only major portion of the Missouri River that has been preserved in a natural and free-flowing state. It provides a remarkable float trip for canoers and rafters, and is suitable for beginners. Along the way, habitats change from rolling grasslands to beautiful white cliffs to rugged badlands. The Evans Bend area, which starts at river mile six on the south side (use your BLM floater's guide) and continues for two miles, is a dense forest of mature cottonwoods that supports deer, wild turkey, Canada geese, and a great blue heron rookery, as well as over 200 species of songbirds. Access to this area is very difficult except by river. The steep rock walls near Eagle Creek (river mile 56) are a good place to look for nesting raptors (especially prairie falcons) and cliff swallows; Canada geese and white pelicans are usually along the river in the summer. Judith Landing (river mile 88.5) has a heron rookery and is also a good place to see eagles, songbirds, and waterfowl. At Holmes Rapid (river mile 91.5), walk along the south side of the river to the sagebrush flat where you'll find a 200-acre prairie dog town. It's a good place to see burrowing owls and coyotes. Near Greasewood Bottom (river mile 109), the ridges and coulees often contain bighorn sheep and mule deer. The best time to view sheep herds is after August. Near Woodhawk Bottom and Cow Island (river miles 127-131), walk the riparian areas and badlands to see both mule and white-tailed deer, pheasants, Canada geese, white pelicans, and beaver. In the Two Calf area (river miles 143-145), look for the prairie elk herd inhabiting the river bottoms of the Charles M. Russell National Wildlife Refuge, as well as bighorn sheep.

Directions: *Take Montana 80 to Fort Benton, the start of the Wild and Scenic portion of the Missouri. The Fred Robinson Bridge, where U.S. 191 crosses the Missouri northeast of Lewistown, marks the end. River maps are available from the BLM.*

Ownership: BLM (538-7461)
Size: 149 miles **Closest Town:** Fort Benton

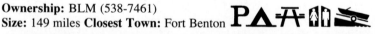

White pelicans are found along many of Montana's larger lakes and rivers, including the Missouri. MICHAEL S. SAMPLE

50 | **Square Butte**

Description: Scenic Square Butte is a volcanic landmark rising some 1,700 feet from the plains of north-central Montana. It has exceptional wildlife values. Deer, pronghorn antelope, and sometimes elk can be seen near the butte, and a herd of about 50 mountain goats can consistently be seen on top. The butte's steep cliffs provide outstanding nesting habitat for raptors; there's a high density of breeding prairie falcons, as well as golden eagles and hawks. Access to Square Butte is available only through the good will of the private landowner, so please be especially courteous. There are instructions and a check-in box at the ranch gate; visitors must ask permission. The road to the butte is sometimes closed during hunting season and is impassable when wet. The unmarked one-mile hike from the end of the road to the top of the butte is quite steep but well worth the view; it takes about an hour.

Directions: Take Montana 80 to Square Butte, then drive west on a county road for 2.5 miles, following the signs to Square Butte Natural Area. Access to the butte is through the headquarters of a private ranch. You can park at the base of the butte and then hike about one mile to reach the top.

Ownership: PVT, BLM (538-7461)
Size: 3,000 acres **Closest Town:** Square Butte

A ferruginous hawk guards her four chicks in their nest along a cliff. Steep, rocky landmarks such as Square Butte provide important nesting sites for raptors on the open plains. KRISTI DUBOIS

51 | **Judith River Wildlife Management Area**

Description: This area of rolling grasslands and ponderosa pine forests serves as a wintering ground for elk and deer from the adjacent Big Belt Mountains. The WMA looks into steep forested canyons with rocky outcroppings. Coyotes, red foxes, long-tailed weasels, badgers, and bobcats are also common mammals. Nearly 100 bird species have been recorded here, including raptors such as golden eagles, Swainson's hawks, goshawks, and great horned owls. Also frequently seen are Clark's nutcracker, Lewis' woodpecker, bluebirds, and western tanagers. Primary access to the WMA is via the road that bisects it. Hiking is possible anywhere except December 1-May 14, when off-road travel is prohibited. Viewing at this time is limited to the road. As you approach the WMA, look for songbirds (especially warblers and vireos), beaver, and waterfowl in the streamside vegetation along the Judith River; this area is private land so view from your car.

Directions: From Lewistown, take U.S. 87 west to Hobson, then take Secondary 239 west to Utica. From Utica, follow the gravel road 12 miles to the south, then turn right onto Yogo Creek Road (after Sapphire Village) and proceed 1.3 miles to the WMA.

Ownership: MDFWP (454-3441)
Size: 5,000 acres **Closest Town:** Utica   **P**

52 | **Big Springs Trout Hatchery**

Description: This state hatchery on beautiful Big Spring Creek provides cutthroat, rainbow, and brown trout, and kokanee salmon to locations all over Montana. The hatchery has its maximum number of fish in the spring—up to 3.5 million. The show pond features white rainbow trout and fish as large as 15 pounds. Take short walks around the hatchery to see Big Spring Creek rising from the ground and to see waterfowl (look for wood ducks in the summer), white-tailed deer, muskrats, beaver, eagles, and belted kingfishers. Viewing is open from daylight to dusk year-round.

Directions: In Lewistown, take First Avenue South. Follow for about seven miles south and turn left at the second hatchery sign.

Ownership: MDFWP (538-5588)
Size: 22.6 acres **Closest Town:** Lewistown   **P⼐**

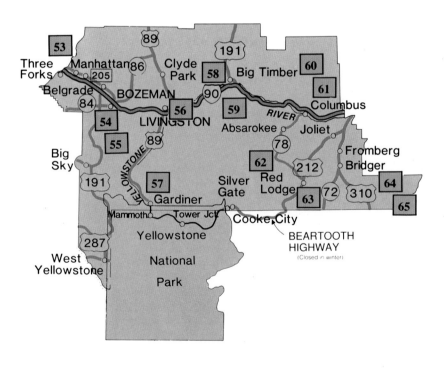

53 | Missouri Headwaters State Park

Description: This is the historic point, made famous by Lewis and Clark, where the Madison, Jefferson, and Gallatin Rivers join to form the Missouri River. This state park has both extensive cottonwood riverbottoms and dry, rocky uplands that give way to limestone cliffs. The Headwaters Trail is a favorite birding site; in the summer, look for Canada geese with goslings, nesting osprey, nighthawks, rock wrens, magpies, and an abundance of warblers and vireos. There's a great blue heron and double-crested cormorant rookery on the Gallatin River, less than a mile upstream from where the rivers join. A hike up Lewis Rock or Fort Rock provides a great view and a good chance to see golden eagles, which nest on nearby cliffs. Prairie falcons are also seen frequently. Marmots and Richardson's ground squirrels can be seen near the rocks, while in the meadows white-tailed deer are common and moose are occasionally seen. Coyotes are heard frequently at night. While river otters are shy and elusive, their sign is consistently found nearby. Beaver and painted turtles are common and rattlesnakes, bullsnakes, and racers all dwell here. Interpretative displays explain about area wildlife and history. A canoe trip is a great way to see wildlife and view or fish for trout.

Directions: *From Interstate 90, exit at Three Forks. Turn east on Secondary 205, then turn north on Secondary 286 and follow for three miles.*

Ownership: MDFWP (994-4042)
Size: 527 acres **Closest Town:** Three Fork

Beaver dams create important habitat for a variety of wildlife, including fish, waterfowl, shorebirds, and even moose. Beaver are common along many streams and rivers in western Montana. MICHAEL S. SAMPLE

| 54 | **Kirk Hill** | *Bozeman*
Urban Site |

Description: This area, managed by the Museum of the Rockies, is a good spot to view wildlife and learn about natural history. There are some excellent signs identifying plants and trees. The area offers both short birdwatching walks and longer hikes on adjacent Gallatin National Forest lands. The trail starts out in a creekbottom area that's loaded with songbirds. It then climbs very steeply for about one-fourth mile into dry, Douglas-fir-covered foothills, where three loop trails from .3 to .6 miles long originate (trail maps are posted at the entrance and at each trail intersection). As you climb further up the hill to a ridge, the habitat changes to small sagebrush meadows. At the southeast corner of the area you can hook up with a national forest trail to Bozeman Creek/Hyalite Creek Divide. More than 70 bird species have been recorded throughout the area; some birds of special interest include Steller's jays, Clark's nutcrackers, lazuli buntings, and great gray owls. Mule deer, elk, and moose are seen occasionally, and black bears use the area. It's a great wildflower area, many of which are identified by signs. Pets, horses, bicycles, and hunting are prohibited. Bird and plant lists and brochures are available at the site or at the Museum of the Rockies.

Directions: *From Bozeman, follow South 19th Avenue directly south for about five miles. As you approach the mountains, the road bears sharply to the right (west); Kirk Hill is on the south side of this sharp curve.*

Ownership: Montana State University (994-5257)
Size: 50 acres **Closest Town:** Bozeman

P

The Steller's jay's irridescent colors can be seen in many Montana areas that have coniferous forests. MICHAEL S. SAMPLE

55 | Palisade Falls

Description: This short nature trail winds through a spruce/fir forest and leads to a stunning waterfall. It's a great family and environmental education area, and is totally accessible to people with disabilities, with interpretative signs in Braille. The .6-mile paved trail has 16 natural history stops, many of which involve wildlife. In this fairly typical western Montana forested habitat you can usually see common species like pine squirrels, northern flickers, red-breasted nuthatches, and mountain chickadees. A 1988 windstorm damaged many large trees, providing good habitat for many of these birds. Also look for western tanagers, warbling vireos, yellow-throated warblers, and ruby-crowned kinglets. A pika colony can be viewed in the rock slide near the scenic falls, where marmots can also be seen. The cliff walls on Palisade Mountain provide nest sites for golden eagles. Look for dippers near the creek, a natural exploration spot for youngsters. Deer, elk, moose, and black bear are sometimes seen near the Hyalite Canyon Road, and the reservoir has waterfowl, osprey, and bald eagles.

Directions: In Bozeman, follow 19th Avenue south out of town for about six miles. Turn left onto Hyalite Canyon Road and travel about 11 miles (past Hyalite Reservoir) until the road forks. Take the left fork (East Fork Hyalite Road) for one mile to Palisade Falls trail.

Ownership: USFS (587-6701)
Size: .6-mile paved trail **Closest Town:** Bozeman

P⊼🏠⛟ ⅄

56 | Sleeping Giant Wildlife Museum

Description: This wildlife museum on the way to Yellowstone National Park features 17 taxidermic displays of North American wildlife in lifelike dioramas appearing as they might in the wild. The centerpiece is a full-scale representation of a buffalo jump—reputedly the nation's only. There's also a grizzly bear display with four bears in a feeding confrontation over a dead bull elk, and a very rare mount of a white bull elk. While most of the displays are of big game species such as mule deer, pronghorn antelope, bighorn sheep, and mountain goats, there are also some good mounts of owls, grouse, hawks, and golden eagles. Signs with each display give useful natural history information. Summer hours are from 8 a.m.-8 p.m.; winter hours are from 9 a.m.-5 p.m. The admission cost is $3 for adults, $2 for children (6-12), and $2.50 for seniors.

Directions: From Interstate 90, exit at Livingston (exit 333) and drive south on U.S. 89 toward Yellowstone Park for .5 mile. The museum is on the west side of the road, marked by a sign with a life-size elk.

Ownership: PVT (222-8719)
Size: 4,000 square feet **Closest Town:** Livingston

P🏠⛟$🚻

57 | Northern Yellowstone Winter Range

Description: This winter range has the largest and most diverse group of hoofed animals in the lower 48 states. The drive route through parts of the Gallatin National Forest and Yellowstone Park is a scenic area of rugged mountains and aspen-dotted foothills. The land between Cinnabar Mountain and the park boundary is privately owned by the Church Universal and Triumphant, and is well posted against trespass. Between December and May, the range is the major wintering area for the Northern Yellowstone elk herd, which at 20,000 is the nation's largest. Mule deer, pronghorn antelope, and an occasional bison add diversity. In the winter, bighorn sheep are consistently found on the dry, open slopes of Cinnabar Mountain (right across the Yellowstone River at Corwin Springs) and are usually close to the road, offering good photo opportunities. The Yellowstone River between Corwin Springs and Gardiner is also an important wintering area for bald eagles; look for their white heads in the tallest trees and snags.

Directions: Take U.S. 89 to Corwin Springs. This is a 12-mile drive route that runs from Corwin Springs to Gardiner, and then on to Jardine. You can either follow U.S. 89 or cross the Yellowstone River at Corwin Springs and head south towards Gardiner on the gravel road. From Gardiner take the county road for about five miles northeast to Jardine.

Ownership: PVT, USFS (848-7375)
Size: 12 miles **Closest Town:** Gardiner

The open hillsides above the Yellowstone River near Gardiner provide critical winter range for elk and many other species. CHRISTOPHER CAUBLE

58 | Yellowstone River Trout Hatchery

Description: This is a brood hatchery for the Yellowstone cutthroat trout, maintaining adult fish (brood) from which eggs are taken to supply production hatcheries (those that raise fish). It's an exceptional place for viewing trout, with three raceways outside that during the summer can have 2,500 or more fish. The largest fish are about 18-26 inches and can weigh up to six pounds. It's particularly interesting to visit between March and May when the eggs are removed. On Tuesdays the fish are checked for "ripe" eggs, and on Wednesdays the eggs are stripped from the fish. The hatchery produces about a million eggs per year; each four-year old female trout produces about 3,000 eggs. During the summer months raceways inside contain 400,000-600,000 fry. In September most of these two- to three-inch fish are deposited via helicopters and airplanes into high mountain lakes. The hatchery is open seven days a week from 8 a.m. to 4:30 p.m.; staff is on hand to answer questions and to lead tours (school groups are welcome). A pamphlet about the hatchery is available. During the summer the outdoor raceways are left open for public viewing in the evening. Behind the hatchery there is a small wetland area that has red-winged blackbird colonies, waterfowl, and deer. Keep an eye open for belted kingfishers looking for an easy meal near the raceways.

Directions: From Interstate 90, take either Big Timber exit to the town center. Turn north on McLeod Street (the main street) and follow for about .5 mile to the hatchery (you will cross the railroad tracks and go down a hill).

Ownership: MDFWP (932-4434)
Size: Nine acres **Closest Town:** Big Timber **P**

59 | Greycliff Prairie Dog Town

Description: This easily accessible state park is the only developed prairie dog viewing area in Montana. The habitat is primarily shortgrass prairie and sagebrush, and the town is usually teeming with black-tailed prairie dogs. The road through the dog town is paved and some excellent signs explain prairie dog ecology and behavior. Shooting is prohibited, but the photo opportunity is exceptional, as the dogs are acclimated to people. Large hawks and golden eagles are sometimes seen looking for a meal, and common prairie songbirds including western meadowlarks, vesper sparrows, horned larks, and mountain bluebirds are frequently seen nearby. Prairie dogs usually are less active from about November to early March, but can be dependably seen the rest of the year unless the weather is excessively cold or hot. You can view the dogs either from the car or by walking through this small area.

Directions: From Interstate 90, take exit 377 about seven miles east of Big Timber. From there, follow the signs to the dog town.

Ownership: MDFWP (252-4654)
Size: 98 acres **Closest Town:** Greycliff **P**

60 | **Hailstone National Wildlife Refuge**

Description: This is a large alkaline lake in wide-open shortgrass prairie country dominated by rocky outcroppings and small grassy hills. This medium-sized refuge is noted primarily for its waterfowl (several thousand during migration times) and shorebirds, commonly including mallards, gadwalls, teal, redheads, canvasbacks, avocets, phalaropes, white pelicans, grebes, and gulls. A good place to view water birds is a small hill that overlooks the lake. Several mudflats near the lake are a good spot for shorebirds. Pronghorn antelope and sharp-tailed grouse are frequently seen in the upland areas, which are vegetated with sagebrush, greasewood, and native grasses. There is a black-tailed prairie dog town on the east side of the lake; watch for golden eagles and hawks preying on the dogs. Peregrine falcons also have been sighted here. Motorized boats are prohibited on the lake.

Directions: Take Secondary 306 to Rapelje. From Rapelje, turn east on a county road and follow for four miles to Hailstone Basin Road. Take this gravel road north for about 1.5 miles to the refuge.

Ownership: USFWS (538-8706)
Size: 1,913 acres **Closest Town:** Rapelje

A black-tailed prairie dog gives the "all-clear" signal. Greycliff Prairie Dog Town east of Big Timber provides the only developed viewing area for prairie dogs in Montana. HARRY ENGELS

67

61 Eastlick Pond/Big Lake Waterfowl Management Area

Description: Eastlick Pond, easily accessible off a fair dirt road, is a very productive prairie pothole that's very popular with Billings-area birdwatchers. Chestnut-collared longspurs, horned larks, water pipits, meadowlarks, red-tailed hawks, harriers, and gulls can often be seen. Waterfowl commonly viewed include widgeons, mallards, and teal. It's a real concentration spot for great blue herons, and there are often large flocks of Canada geese in the spring and fall. Shorebirds seen here include sandpipers and long-billed curlews. There's a black-tailed prairie dog town across the road from the pond, and it's a very dependable place to see nesting burrowing owls in the summer (also look near the top of the hill on the same side of the road as the pond). The shelterbelt of trees a short distance north of the pond often holds small birds such as warblers, Say's phoebe, barn swallows, goldfinches, and ruby-crowned kinglets. Big Lake is a large alkaline lake that's a great place to see ducks, geese, and shorebirds—when there's water. In the spring and in wet years it's usually good for white pelicans and tundra swans during migration as well as cormorants and gulls. Shorebirds found here include black-necked stilts, black-bellied plovers, yellowlegs, avocets, and phalaropes. It's a good place for the unusual—look for scoters and peregrine falcons. In late April or early May you often will see more than 50 bird species on the drive to Eastlick Pond and Big Lake.

Directions: In Billings, follow Rimrock Road to Secondary 302 and then drive toward Molt approximately 21 miles. Just before you reach Molt, turn left (due west) on the dirt road (Eastlick Road) and follow for about one mile. Turn right onto Lakeview Road and proceed a short distance to Eastlick Pond on the right (known to local birders as Corral Pond). To reach Big Lake from here, continue north on Lakeview Road until you hit the Molt-Rapelje Road. Turn left (west) on this road and drive 4.7 miles. At an old church, turn left on Wheat Basin Road and drive another 1.1 miles to Big Lake (a total of 9.1 miles from Eastlick Pond).

Ownership: PVT, MDFWP (252-4654)
Size: Big Lake—701 acres **Closest Town:** Molt

Abundant wildflowers at Jimmy Joe Campground attract a variety of butterflies, including swallowtails.
MICHAEL S. SAMPLE

| **62** | **Jimmy Joe Campground** |

Description: The profusion of spring and summer wildflowers attracts an array of butterflies at this picturesque campground near the rugged Beartooth Mountains and East Rosebud River. Look for a large bed of the kinnikinnick plant (it's close to the ground with green, shiny leaves) in May and early June where the campground road joins the main road at the south end. This plant provides nectar for hairstreak, elfin, and blue butterflies. In June, mourning cloak, Weidemeyer's admiral, angle wing, and blue butterflies can be found patrolling the campground road. In late June and July the pink dogbane flowers lining the paved canyon road provide nectar for about 20 species of butterflies and skippers. Later in the year, while there are fewer species, you can still find angle wings, sulfurs, and lesser frittillaries, and a new crop of mourning cloaks. Mule and white-tailed deer and moose are sometimes seen near the road, and the campground itself is a good birding area.

Directions: *Take Montana 78 to Roscoe, then follow signs to East Rosebud Lake for about nine miles south on a good gravel road. Jimmy Joe Campground is about five miles before the lake and is well signed.*

Ownership: USFS (446-2103)
Size: Ten acres **Closest Town:** Roscoe **PΔⱭ̄Ɑ̄**

| **63** | **Meeteetse Trail** |

Description: The habitats along this drive change dramatically from riverbottom to mountains to arid prairie, and feature large rock spires, rolling foothills with aspen groves, willow-lined ponds, and near-desert sagebrush flats. The wildlife viewing here is equally diverse. Look for beaver, white-tailed deer, moose, and a variety of songbirds along the first four miles of the trail immediately after crossing Rock Creek. Mule deer and an occasional black bear can be seen as the trail climbs into the more mountainous habitat, while golden eagles and red-tailed hawks often soar overhead. Moving into the drier prairie, look for coyotes, foxes, and badgers. Sage grouse and pronghorn antelope can be seen on the sagebrush flats. There are trails along the North and South Forks of Grove Creek, but hiking is possible on any of the nearby public land. The road isn't plowed in the winter, but cross-country skiing is possible (snow permitting). The northern portions of the road pass through deer and elk winter range. Mountain bicycling also has excellent potential in season.

Directions: *From Red Lodge, drive one mile south on U.S. 212. Just before you reach the USFS Ranger Station, take a dirt road going southeast. This is the start of the 19-mile drive route, which ends where Meeteetse Trail hits Secondary 72 south of Belfry. Note: about a mile from the turnoff after crossing Rock Creek, bear left and proceed up the hill.*

Ownership: PVT, BLM (657-6262)
Size: 19 miles **Closest Town:** Red Lodge

Description: This scenic drive route passes through high plateaus, spectacular canyons, and thick Douglas-fir forests. There's good birding along Sage Creek and in the canyons; look for sage thrashers, kestrels, rock wrens, ruby-crowned kinglets, and warblers. The Sage Creek Campground is notable both for its hummingbirds and its green-tailed towhees. Mule deer are numerous in the forested areas and black bears are occasionally seen. Driving on toward the Big Ice Cave, look for bats roosting along the limestone cliffs; blue grouse are often seen near the road. There's a small elk herd here, but it's infrequently seen. The drive route ends at Dry Head Vista, a barren plateau with a stunning view that's a good place to see raptors—especially golden eagles. You can hike anywhere along the route, but for an interesting short walk, drive down the Crooked Creek Road until it hits Wyoming Creek. From here, a ten-minute walk on an unmarked trail following Wyoming Creek to the bottom of Crooked Creek is a good all-around viewing area. For a longer hike (it's a steep hike with no trail and takes about an hour), cross the creek and head up Commissary Ridge. The open ridge top provides a great view of the Pryor Mountains Wild Horse Range, where you'll see horses about half the time. A hike in the wild country of Lost Water Canyon provides a good chance to see wild horses. The drive through this area is impassable in wet weather; high-clearance vehicles are helpful. This is very remote country, so take caution. This area has good potential for mountain bicycling in the summer and cross-country skiing in the winter.

Directions: From Bridger, take U.S. 310 south for about two miles. Turn left (east) onto Pryor Mountain Road and proceed about 15 miles until you reach Sage Creek. Continue east along Sage Creek (FS Road 3085); from here it's about seven miles to the Sage Creek Campground. This wildlife viewing drive route extends from the Sage Creek Campground to the Dry Head Vista.

Ownership: Crow Indian Reservation, USFS (657-6361)
Size: 77,000 acres **Closest Town:** Pryor

A red fox pup pauses at the entrance to its den. Though seldom seen, red foxes range throughout much of Montana. MICHAEL S. SAMPLE

65   **Bad Pass Road**

Description: Bighorn Canyon is Montana's most spectacular canyon area, with white sand hills, colorful canyons with cliffs up to 2,000 feet high, and prairie grasslands. The Bad Pass Road is a 25-mile drive route on a paved highway that passes through the 30,000-acre Pryor Mountain Wild Horse Range. This sanctuary for about 125 wild horses is managed by the Bureau of Land Management. In the fall and spring, bighorn sheep are often visible close to the road, especially near the Devil Canyon Overlook. Mule deer and raptors are common residents of the Canyon, as well as over 200 bird species. The Bighorn Canyon Visitor Center near Lovell has maps of the park as well as exhibits. Hiking is possible almost anywhere; a good bet is the trail that starts behind the Hough Creek Ranger Station. It passes through a juniper woodland area leading into a canyon and a natural spring, and is a good place to see both wild horses and bighorn sheep. Another great way to see the canyon and its wildlife is a boat ride tour that leaves from Horseshoe Bend.

Directions: *Take U.S. 310 south to Lovell, Wyoming, then follow U.S. 14A a short distance until it joins Wyoming 37. Turn north onto Wyoming 37 (Bad Pass Road). This is the start of the 25-mile drive route, which ends at Barry's Landing.*

Ownership: NPS (666-2412)
Size: 120,000 acres
Closest Town: Lovell, Wyoming

Certain types of wildlife viewing demand caution. Rattlesnakes may be encountered in many areas, but especially around rocky outcroppings in central and eastern Montana.
HANK FISCHER

71

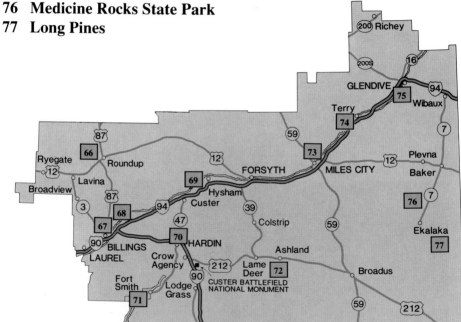

66 Lake Mason National Wildlife Refuge

Description: The reeds, cattails, and mudflats of this productive, extensive prairie marsh attracts large nesting populations of both waterfowl (mallards, gadwalls, teal, pintails) and shorebirds (yellowlegs, American avocets, phalaropes, upland sandpipers, willets)—except during very dry years. Large numbers of migrating Canada geese, gulls, and white pelicans can be seen in the spring and fall, and migrating bald eagles and peregrine falcons are occasionally seen. Several pronghorn antelope herds roam the drier uplands around the lake, and a black-tailed prairie dog town can be found along its southeastern edge. Burrowing owls use the dog holes for their nests. Watch for coyotes, red fox, and an occasional bobcat preying on the prairie dogs. Prairie rattlesnakes and horned lizards can also be seen here. A portion of the refuge (primarily the north and east sections) is closed to public access, but the rest of the refuge is open to hiking and non-motorized boating.

Directions: *From Roundup, take U.S. 87 (Main Street) to 13th Avenue. Turn west and follow for one block, then turn west onto Golf Course Road. Follow this road for 6.5 miles, then turn right and proceed north for about three miles to Lake Mason. A high-clearance vehicle is recommended.*

Ownership: USFWS (538-8706)
Size: 16,830 acres **Closest Town:** Roundup

P

67 Two Moon Park
Billings Urban Site

Description: This Yellowstone River park is a top local birding spot, with nearly 200 species recorded. It's a riverbottom habitat, with cottonwood trees and dense underbrush interspersed with backwater sloughs that have reeds and cattails. A slough along the north side of the park is a dependable place to see waterfowl and beaver, with thick vegetation allowing a stealthy approach. You can see nesting wood ducks in spring and summer and, since the slough usually doesn't freeze, waterfowl of all kinds in the winter. Look for bald eagles in the winter and spring, and migrating warblers (including Townsend's, Nashville, and blackpoll), orioles, and black-headed grosbeaks also in the spring. There are nesting pairs of both screech owls and great horned owls in the park, and Canada geese and white pelicans along the river. Mammals often spotted include white-tailed deer, raccoon, and red fox. Several unmarked trails crisscross the area, and a designated nature trail with six marked posts circles the park. Cross-country skiing is possible when there's adequate snow. A brochure describing the nature trail is available at the caretaker's home. The park is open from a half-hour before sunrise to 10 p.m.

Directions: *In Billings, take Bench Boulevard off Main Street (U.S. 87) , and then make the first right turn (about 5 mile) onto a gravel road. The park entrance is at the bottom of the hill.*

Ownership: Yellowstone County (256-2703)
Size: 150 acres **Closest Town:** Billings

P

The mountain bluebird has been called "the bird that carries the sky on its back." It usually relies on tree cavities for nesting, but in many open areas of Montana, bird houses have been placed on fences to attract these insect-eating songbirds. STEVE WIRT

68 Shepherd Ah-Nei

Description: This area's rolling hills and eroded gullies dotted with sandstone escarpments are largely covered with open grasslands and sagebrush, with some ponderosa pine and juniper. It's a great area to see mule deer and an occasional pronghorn antelope. Small mammals such as Richardson's ground squirrels and white-tailed jackrabbits are common, and form the prey base for golden eagles and coyotes. It's also a good place to see sharp-tailed grouse, meadowlarks, northern shrikes, magpies, and a bevy of songbirds. Look for kestrels and red-tailed hawks in the summer and rough-legged hawks in the winter. This area has historically been an important enviromental educational site for Billings area schools. Its excellent nature trail is a mile-long loop; for a longer walk, take one of many undeveloped side trails. The area east of the road is closed to motorized vehicles, creating a pleasant place for a quiet walk.

Directions: *From Shepherd, follow Shepherd Road north for two miles. Turn right (east) and proceed 2.5 miles to C.A. Road. Turn north on this road and drive about six miles to a small parking area on the east side of the road (there's a parking lot on the west side of the road about a mile sooner). Follow the one-mile long nature trail on the east side (right) of the road.*

Ownership: BLM (657-6262)
Size: 4,016 acres **Closest Town:** Shepherd

P

69 Howrey Island

Description: This primitive, isolated Yellowstone River bottom area is densely forested with cottonwoods and willows but dotted with occasional small meadows. The island is quite wild, with no established trails; navigating through the dense underbrush can be a challenge. The best bet is to follow the old vehicle tracks and deer trails. The island is exceptional for birdwatching, especially for bald eagles (common in the summer with even larger populations in the winter), red-tailed hawks, great horned owls, red-headed woodpeckers, warblers, great blue herons, and even turkeys. This part of the Yellowstone River is closed to waterfowl hunting, and concentrations of ducks and geese are often quite high. Wood ducks are common, and white-tailed deer are abundant. Also look for red fox, beaver, and fox squirrels. Motorized access to the island is restricted. A nearby wildlife viewing spot is the Isaac Homestead, about a mile to the north of Howery's Island, just across the bridge over the Yellowstone River. The walking is somewhat easier here, and it can be a good place to find asparagus in the spring.

Directions: *Take Interstate 94 to Hysham, then follow Secondary 311 west for 6.9 miles to the Myers Bridge fishing access site turnoff. Proceed a short distance past the fishing access site to a dry river channel; you can park here and walk to the island.*

Ownership: MDFWP, BLM (232-7000)
Size: 580 acres **Closest Town:** Hysham

P

70 Grant Marsh Wildlife Management Area

Description: This is a small, very accessible riverbottom area with cottonwood trees and grassy meadows that lies along the Bighorn River. It's a good birding spot, especially for waterfowl and songbirds. One of the best viewing places is the long, narrow cattail marsh that runs from the WMA entrance to the river. Walk or drive along the edge of the marsh to view red-winged blackbirds, teal, and mallards. Flickers and downy woodpeckers can also be seen here. Warblers, vireos, and thrushes can be found near the brushy vegetation (especially during migration) while the grassy meadows are the best place to see white-tailed deer and pheasants. The river is a good spot for ducks and Canada geese (especially during migration), and great blue heron, mink, muskrat, and beaver can be seen along the river banks. In the winter, bald eagles are usually quite common. This area is fairly small, so it's easy to cover in an hour or two.

Directions: Take Interstate 90 to Hardin, then follow Montana 47 north for 6.8 miles. Turn right (east) onto a good gravel road at the sign for Grant Marsh. Continue east for one mile to the beginning of the WMA.

Ownership: MDFWP (252-4654)
Size: 140 acres **Closest Town**: Hardin **P** 🚶

71 Yellowtail Dam Afterbay

Description: This is an approximately two-mile long body of water immediately below Yellowtail Dam, created by the much smaller Afterbay dam. The water here seldom freezes, attracting an outstanding concentration of wintering waterfowl. While ducks and Canada geese can be seen most of the year, thousands of birds arrive in the winter. As many as 47 bird species have been recorded on the river, commonly including green-winged teal, mallards, redheads, canvasbacks, ringnecks, Barrow's goldeneyes, hooded mergansers, grebes, and cormorants as well as oldsquaw (an ocean duck rarely seen in Montana). Afterbay and the nearby portions of the Bighorn River may sustain as many 20,000 wintering mallards. Avian predators of the waterfowl include bald eagles in the winter (some nest nearby and can be seen all year), merlins, rough-legged hawks, prairie falcons, and an occasional peregrine falcon. Tundra swans, white pelicans, common loons, and sandhill cranes may also appear during migration, as well as spotted sandpipers, killdeer, American avocets, and Wilson's phalaropes. There isn't much need for walking here—just bring binoculars and a spotting scope.

Directions: From Hardin, take Secondary 313 to Fort Smith. The Afterbay can be viewed from either the northside (cross the river at the Afterbay Dam) or the southside road and campground.

Ownership: NPS (666-2412) **P**
Closest Town: Fort Smith

72 Black's Pond Drive Route

Description: This 23-mile Custer National Forest drive route circles around a timbered plateau that arises from the surrounding prairie. The ponderosa pine forest is interspersed with rugged breaks, creeks and ponds, and sagebrush flats. Black's Pond is a good place to see deer, wild turkeys, and songbirds. On the way in, the streambottoms along Cow Creek and O'Dell Creek are a good place to look for warblers, nuthatches, western tanagers, orioles, golden eagles, merlins, and kestrels. Near the junction of Cow Creek Road (FS Road 95) and O'Dell Creek Road (FS Road 131), watch for sharp-tailed grouse (there's a dancing ground near the junction of FS Roads 95 and 794) and wild turkeys. Pronghorn antelope are common on the open prairie, where mule and white-tailed deer are also present. Coyotes are seen frequently. Six bat species have been identified in the area, including the rare pallid bat; look for bats in the evening near Black's Pond, O'Dell Reservoir, and Cow Creek Reservoir. While there are no marked trails, hiking is possible almost anywhere. The roads can be impassable in wet weather, but bicycling and skiing are both good options in season. At Poker Jim Butte, a short distance off the drive route, there's a lookout with an exceptional view and a picnic area.

Directions: *From Ashland, proceed east on U.S. 212 for three miles, then follow Otter Creek Road (Secondary 484) south for 19 miles to Cow Creek Road (FS Road 95). The drive route begins here. Follow Cow Creek Road for five miles, and from there take a loop trip. Turn right (north) on FS Road 131, travel three miles and take FS Road 3021 (Stocker Branch Road) to Black's Pond. Continue up FS Road 3021 about two miles and turn southwest (left) on FS Road 802. Go about two miles (past O'Dell Reservoir) and take a left on FS Road 801. Follow this southeast for two miles, then take a left (east) and go back along Cow Creek Road (FS Road 95), which you follow back out to the Otter Creek Road (you'll retrace the last five miles).*

Ownership: USFS (784-2344)
Size: 44,800 acres **Closest Town**: Ashland

Muskrats are common residents of Montana marshes, ponds, and rivers. MICHAEL S. SAMPLE

| 73 | **Pirogue Island** | *Miles City*
Urban Site |

Description: This cottonwood-covered Yellowstone River island with dense areas of Russian olive and willow as well as open meadows and hay fields is easily accessible by good dirt roads. Look for songbirds (warblers, brown thrashers, kingbirds) and pheasants in the thick underbrush, and look for woodpeckers (downy, hairy, and also flickers) and orioles in the mature cottonwood trees. When runoff or precipitation is heavy, the sloughs and old river channels usually attract waterfowl—especially mallards, teal, and wood ducks. White-tailed deer are common throughout the island, while beaver work is usually seen along the river banks. Near the main channel of the Yellowstone River look for ducks, geese, and white pelicans. Great blue herons and cormorants can be seen fairly dependably in the summer, and bald eagles are common in the late fall and winter. The best way to see the island is to park your car at the entrance and walk on the old dirt roads that traverse the area.

Directions: From Miles City, go one mile north on Montana 59. Turn right onto Kinsey Road and drive 1.5 miles east, then take another right (south) onto a good gravel road and proceed 1.6 miles to Pirogue Island.

Ownership: MDFWP (232-4365)
Size: 269 acres **Closest Town:** Miles City **P** 🚶

| 74 | **Terry Badlands** |

Description: These badlands immediately adjacent to the Yellowstone River are extremely rugged and beautiful. The deep chasms make walking difficult, but the badland bluffs, mixed grasses, juniper, and ponderosa pine provide great wildlife habitat. Racers, bull snakes, and rattlesnakes can be found here, and pronghorn antelope, mule deer, coyotes, and foxes are common. Golden eagles nest in the area and are seen frequently; other common nesting raptors include great horned owls and prairie falcons (look for cavities in the sandstone ledges). The raptors prey on the ever-abundant desert cottontails and white-tailed jackrabbits. Birds of special interest here include mockingbirds, Sprague's pipit, mountain plover, long-billed curlews, and upland sandpipers. A walk along the bluffs on either side of the overlook offers opportunities to see pinon jays, western tanagers, and western meadowlarks. You can hike in from the overlook, but a better bet is to follow an old vehicle track about a mile east of the overlook, right off the dirt road you came in on (look for wilderness study area signs). The dirt roads here can be good for mountain bicycling.

Directions: Take Interstate 94 to Terry, then follow Secondary 253 north for about two miles. Turn left onto a fair dirt road and head west for six miles to a scenic overlook. The road is impassable when wet.

Ownership: BLM (232-7000)
Size: 43,000 acres **Closest Town:** Terry 🚶 🚲

75 | Makoshika State Park

Description: This desolate badlands area features buttes, pinnacles, and spires that have eroded into fascinating shapes. While the climate is desert-like and the weather often extreme, the park hosts an impressive array of wildlife including mule deer and coyotes. From April 15-October 15, as many as 50 turkey vultures can be seen; look near Radio Hill and at the Buzzard Ridge View Point. Golden eagles, kestrels, prairie falcons, and red-tailed hawks can often be spotted circling overhead looking for prey. Look for Brewer's and vesper sparrows nesting in or under sagebrush. Other common birds are horned larks, western meadowlarks, and lark sparrows. McCarty Pond and Spring is usually a good viewing area. Reptiles to look for include horned lizards (horned toads), bull snakes, and prairie rattlesnakes. For an excellent .6 mile walk through some unique geological features, take the Cap Rock Nature Trail—a good place to see rock wrens and turkey vultures. An auto tour booklet is available at the park.

Directions: *Take Interstate 94 to Glendive. The park is two miles southeast of Glendive on Snyder Avenue; look for signs as you enter town.*

Ownership: MDFWP (365-8596)
Size: 8,834 acres **Closest Town**: Glendive $P \triangle \mathreverse{\pi} \$$

76 | Medicine Rocks State Park

Description: The unique sandstone rock formations at this park are surrounded by prairie grasslands and ponderosa pine forests. Teddy Roosevelt once said it is "as fantastically beautiful a place as I've ever seen." It's an excellent area to see raptors of all kinds—red-tailed hawks, kestrels, northern harriers, and ferruginous hawks. Golden eagles, merlins, prairie falcons, and cliff swallows nest on the cliffs. The prairie grasslands hold sharp-tailed grouse and a variety of songbirds (meadowlarks, mountain bluebirds, rufous-sided towhees, red-breasted nuthatches). Mule deer and pronghorn antelope are frequently seen. There is a large prairie dog town just west of the park, and red fox and coyotes are sometimes seen hunting on the town. A short loop road around the park provides opportunities to view wildlife and the sandstone buttes. The Eagle Rock and Castle Rock areas are good for short walks. Look for horned lizards, bull snakes, and prairie rattlesnakes.

Directions: *From Baker, follow Montana 7 south for 25 miles.*

Ownership: BLM, MDFWP (232-4365) $P \triangle \mathreverse{\pi} \blacksquare\blacksquare$
Size: 316 acres **Closest Town**: Ekalaka

 The most widespread and abundant mammal in Montana is the deer mouse. It's found in all habitats across the state.

| 77 | **Long Pines** |

Description: This area's ponderosa pine forests and aspen-lined draws are interspersed with sagebrush prairie and rocky, rolling hills. A fire burned over much of this area in 1988, creating new wildlife habitat (woodpeckers and bluebirds are especially abundant). It's a good place to see raptors, especially golden eagles and the nation's highest reported nesting density of merlins. Look for merlins hunting in the meadows and along the cliff edges—also a good place to see great horned owls, kestrels, and rough-legged hawks. Capitol Rock is an excellent place to look for golden eagles, while Abrogast Way Trail, a short distance to the northwest, is a good place to walk and see white-tailed deer. A few nearby springs host warblers and other songbirds. Long Pines birdwatchers should look for turkeys and a variety of songbirds; of special interest are ovenbirds and peewees. Coyotes can be heard howling in the evenings and foxes can occasionally be seen. In the prairie areas look for rattlesnakes, bull snakes, and meadowlarks. Cross-country skiing is sometimes possible in the winter, when viewing for bald eagles, turkeys, and white-tailed deer is excellent. Just north of Long Pines, Ekalaka Hills is a beautiful open meadows surrounded by ponderosa pines, and is a good place to see wild turkeys, hawks, and eagles. From the Camp Needmore entrance (just off Secondary 323), continue along the Rimrock Carter Road until you reach Stagville Draw on Secondary 323. This area is a mix of public and private land; be aware of trespass.

Directions: From Ekalaka, take Secondary 323 for about 17 miles south to Belltower, then head southeast on FS Road 818 and travel the width of the Custer National Forest. This 12-mile drive route starts on the west boundary of the forest and ends on the east boundary, not far from Capitol Rock.

Ownership: USFS (605-797-4432)
Size: 19,200 acres **Closest Town**: Camp Crook, SD   **PA**   🚶⛷🚴

The distinctive cliffs of Medicine Rocks State Park provide nesting areas for eagles, hawks, and falcons, while the surrounding grassland supports sharp-tailed grouse, mule deer, coyotes, and numerous other species. KRISTI DUBOIS

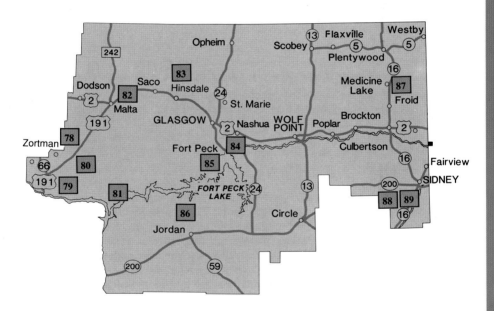

| 78 | **Little Rocky Mountains** |

Description: This heavily timbered, isolated mountain range rises abruptly from the surrounding plains, providing habitat for a unique mix of mountain and prairie wildlife. Many species found infrequently in eastern Montana are found here. See bighorn sheep (especially in winter) on the south side of Saddle Butte and Silver Peak as well as Lewis' woodpeckers and white-throated swifts. Look for blue grouse along Pony Gulch; violet-green swallows can also be seen. Hike up Old Scraggy Peak from Beaver Creek to see mule and white-tailed deer, coyotes, beavers, and porcupines. The Camp Creek Campground is very popular with birdwatchers—look for warblers, Clark's nutcrackers, and mountain chickadees. In the winter watch for Bohemian waxwings here, evening grosbeaks in Zortman, and rosy finches on the steep slopes. In the spring look for nesting prairie falcons on Silver Peak's southern cliffs, and golden eagles on the drive in. Mining and logging roads provide access, but watch for trucks and machinery. Cross-country skiing is usually good. Information and maps are available from the BLM office in Zortman (open June-August).

Directions: From Malta, take U.S. 191 about 40 miles southwest, then follow a good county road towards Zortman for seven miles, turning at the Camp Creek Campground turnoff.

Ownership: BLM (654-1240)
Size: 29,570 acres **Closest Town**: Zortman **P⊼⛺🏠**   🚶🚴🎿

| 79 | **Charles M. Russell National Wildlife Refuge Tour Route** |

Description: This exceptional car tour passes through prairie grasslands, dense ponderosa pines, and thick sagebrush, with views of the scenic Missouri River. The Charles M. Russell National Wildlife Refuge—third largest refuge in the contiguous United States—is probably the wildest remaining remnant of the Northern Great Plains, and contains the full complement of prairie wildlife: mule and white-tailed deer, sharp-tailed grouse, prairie dogs, pronghorn antelope, and many varieties of hawks and eagles. Tour highlights vary with the season; from mid-March through mid-May, view sharp-tailed grouse performing their unusual mating dances, about half-way through the route at post #10. In September, see and hear the nation's largest remaining prairie elk herd (nearly 1,000 animals) performing its fall mating rituals on the southern part of the tour route, along the Missouri River. It's second only to Yellowstone Park for elk viewing. No human entry is permitted to this area, but the elk can be easily seen and photographed from the road. Hiking is possible almost anywhere else. See ducks and Canada geese, raptors, deer, and elk on the Jones Island footpath, along the Missouri River at the southern end of the route.

Directions: This approximately two-hour, 20-mile auto tour route begins and ends on U.S. 191. The north entrance is 55 miles from Malta; the south entrance is a half mile north of where U.S. 191 crosses the Missouri. The graveled road can be bad when wet.

Ownership: USFWS (538-8706)
Size: 1.1 million acres **Closest Town**: Lewistown **P⊼⛺**   🚶

Although pronghorn antelope populations were reduced to a few thousand in the 1920s, conservation efforts spurred a rebound. Today, pronghorns in Montana number more than 100,000. Most are found in the eastern half of the state, including such areas as the Charles M. Russell National Wildlife Refuge. MICHAEL S. SAMPLE

80   Manning Corral Prairie Dog Town

Description: This extensive black-tailed prairie dog town, located on the Charles M. Russell National Wildlife Refuge, is a starkly beautiful prairie grassland dissected by steep gullies. There are probably more pairie dogs in this one town than there are humans within a 100-mile radius. Prairie dogs have a complex social system that can be easily observed with a pair of binoculars. The dog town also attracts predators like eagles, hawks, coyotes, bobcats, and badgers. It's a dependable place to see mountain plovers (midsummer is best) and sometimes burrowing owls. Mule deer and pronghorn are usually seen as well. This dog town ranks very high nationally as a site for the reintroduction of the endangered black-footed ferret.

Directions: From Malta, drive about 44 miles south on U.S. 191 to a dirt road heading east, immediately across the road from the Zortman turnoff. Take the right fork and follow the signs first toward Lark Reservoir and then Gullwing Reservoir. Do not take the final turnoff to Gullwing; instead, proceed straight for about one mile to the refuge boundary and the dog town. These fair dirt roads are completely impassable when wet.

Ownership: USFWS (538-8706)
Size*:* 1,000 acres **Closest Town: Zortman

81   UL Bend National Wildlife Refuge

Description: This very remote refuge—it's largely a designated wilderness—features rolling prairie grasslands that give way to steep breaks adjacent to Fort Peck Reservoir. The extensive prairie dog towns attract coyotes, badgers, burrowing owls, golden eagles, ferruginous hawks, and during fall migration, merlins. The Hawley Flat area (near Road 319) is one of the state's best places to find burrowing owls, as well as prairie rattlesnakes and elk. The Valentine Creek area (along Road 416) is a good spot to see sage grouse; observe their mating rituals at the dancing grounds in the spring. For dependable bighorn sheep viewing, take Road 418 to its end and hike up either Brandon Butte or Mickey Butte—both are spectacular. Mountain bicycling is possible on much of UL Bend, but watch out for prickly pear cactus.

Directions: From Malta, follow U.S. 191 south for 24 miles to Dry Fork Road, turn south, and drive 15 miles. Enter the refuge on Route 212, continue south for 1.5 miles, then turn east (left) onto Route 201 into the UL Bend area. A refuge map is needed; pick one up at administrative sites in Lewistown, Fort Peck, Sand Creek, and Jordan. The roads are often impassable when wet; four-wheel drive is recommended.

Ownership: USFWS (538-8706)
Size: 56,049 acres   **Closest Town:** Zortman

 Sage grouse are the largest grouse in North America. Large males can weigh five to seven pounds. They are found in eastern and south-western Montana in large, open areas covered with sagebrush.

82	Bowdoin National Wildlife Refuge

Description: This refuge, which consists mainly of shortgrass prairie, wetlands, scattered shelterbelts, and shrubfields, offers exceptional viewing for waterfowl and white pelicans. See up to 100,000 ducks and geese during migration times. The refuge is especially known for its colonies of nesting birds—Franklin's gulls, black-crowned night herons, and white-faced ibis nest in the bullrush marshes, while white pelicans, double-crested cormorants, and the California and ring-billed gulls occupy several islands. Common upland birds include sharp-tailed grouse, ring-necked pheasants and gray partridge. On Big Island (actually a peninsula), hike to see sharp-tailed grouse mating rituals in April and May (inquire at the refuge headquarters) as well as the best view of some of the more than 1,700 pelicans that nest here. Common large mammals on the refuge include pronghorns, coyotes, and white-tailed deer. More than 236 bird species have been seen here, including notable Montana species like Sprague's pipit and McCown's longspur. Canoeing on the main lake or the Drumbo unit is exceptional, but check with the refuge headquarters for closure dates. An auto tour route (leaflet available on the site) is always open unless bad weather makes the dirt road impassable.

Directions: From Malta, follow U.S. 2 east for about one mile, then drive east on old U.S. 2 for about six miles.

Ownership: USFWS (654-2863)
Size: 15,500 acres Closest Town: Malta

83	Bitter Creek

Description: This area contains some of Montana's finest prairie wilderness, both rugged badlands and open plains. The eastern part of this large roadless area is mostly scenic, as occasional springs foster the growth of cottonwood and aspen stands that support white-tailed deer and a variety of songbirds. Mule deer and pronghorn antelope are also abundant, especially in the winter. Sharp-tailed grouse thrive in the brushy coulees and sage grouse dwell in the silver sage areas on the benchlands. Several reservoirs have been constructed that have waterfowl nesting islands; Flat and Jug Reservoirs are both fairly accessible in the north. Hiking is possible almost anywhere; walk through Eagle's Nest Coulee to see nesting prairie falcons and ferruginous hawks as well as a prairie dog town that's just south of the coulee.

Directions: Take U.S. 2 to about five miles east of Hinsdale, then turn north on Britsch Road (directly opposite Vandalia Road) and follow for about 17 miles. The road is impassable when wet.

Ownership: BLM (228-4316)
Size: 59,660 acres **Closest Town:** Hinsdale

84 | Missouri River/Downstream Recreation Area

Description: This area below Fort Peck Reservoir is a remarkable mix of man-made and natural habitats, including ponds, cottonwood bottoms, and willow thickets. Over 250 birds have been seen in the Fort Peck area, and the reservoir always accounts for some unusual sightings. Waterfowl and gulls are abundant on the ponds below the dam. Glaucous and Thayer's gulls are regular visitors, and three different species of loons have been seen here. Waterfowl include surf scoters, Barrow's goldeneyes, oldsquaws, snow geese, and wood ducks. Piping plovers are frequently seen near the reservoir by the dam. In the Downstream area, look for migrating warblers on the Beaver Creek Nature Trail in Kiwanis Park. There's also an eagle concentration in late fall. The Leo B. Coleman Wildlife Exhibit, just south of the dredge cuts, has bison, elk, and deer. See sharp-tailed grouse mating rituals from late March to May near Flat Lake; take Montana 24 east from the dam and look for a sign to the lake.

Directions: Directly below the Fort Peck power plants, reach the Missouri River by several roads. Reach the Downstream area by turning north off Montana 117 about two miles west of the plants. The dredge cuts are just north of Fort Peck along Montana 117.

Ownership: MDFWP, USFWS, ACE (526-3411)
Size: 1,205 acres
Closest Town: Fort Peck

85 | The Pines Recreation Area

Description: Beautiful ponderosa pines carpet the rugged hills that dip into Fort Peck Reservoir here. A prairie elk herd numbers about 50 animals, mule deer are abundant, coyotes are common, and red fox are occasionally seen. Common songbirds include mountain bluebirds, red-breasted nuthatches, black-capped chickadees, and during migration, a full range of warblers. The mud flats adjacent to the reservoir are exceptional for viewing shorebirds (spotted sandpipers, marbled godwits, greater and lesser yellowlegs). Nesting osprey are common and visible, while bald and golden eagles, prairie falcons, ferruginous hawks, and Swainson's hawks are occasionally seen. Boat along the reservoir shore to see white pelicans, gulls, and waterfowl. In the spring (April-May) view sage grouse mating rituals very near the Pines. Follow Willow Creek Road four miles past the Pines turnoff; look for grouse in the large cactus flat near the junction with TC access road. These roads can be impassable when wet.

Directions: From Fort Peck, follow Montana 24 north for about five miles to The Pines Recreation Area turnoff. Follow the signs; it's 26 miles from the turnoff to the area.

Ownership: ACE (526-3411)
Size: 1,080 acres
Closest Town: Fort Peck

86   Jordan to Hell Creek Drive Route

Description: This drive passes through sagebrush grasslands with deep draws and coulees. In the early morning and late afternoon watch for wild turkeys near the road, as well as sage and sharp-tailed grouse, which mate in the spring (April and May). Pronghorn antelope, mule deer, and golden eagles are common. At the end of the road immediately adjacent to Fort Peck Reservoir, Hell Creek State Recreation Area's scattered ponderosa pine and limber pine is a good place to see elk and a variety of songbirds (horned larks, thrashers, kingbirds, western meadowlarks). In the bay along the reservoir it's easy to spot nesting osprey, white pelicans, and Canada geese. During migration, it's good for viewing common loons.

Directions: Take Montana 200 to Jordan (milepost 213). Turn north on the county road and follow for 26 miles.

Ownership: County Road, MDFWP (232-4365)
Size: 26 miles **Closest Town:** Jordan

87   Medicine Lake National Wildlife Refuge

Description: Although remote and poorly known, this refuge is one of the most outstanding places in Montana to view and photograph birds and mammals. The area consists of rolling plains, small wetlands, shrublands, and a large lake with islands. As many as 100,000 ducks and geese migrate through here, and more than 2,000 white pelicans nest here, primarily on the Big Island. Other islands have nesting populations of cormorants, great blue herons, California gulls, and ring-billed gulls. Thousands of sandhill cranes migrate through this area in late October, and occasionally an endangered whooping crane lands here. The curious courtship rituals of a large population of nesting grebes (both western and Clark's) provide exceptional spring viewing. Try near where Montana 16 crosses the west end of the lake. Look for least terns and piping plovers from mid-May to early August along the gravel beaches on the east and south sides of Medicine and Gaffney Lakes. Pronghorns and white-tailed deer are common on the uplands. The refuge offers exceptional hiking, as nearly a third of it is designated wilderness (the Sandhills area is especially good). There's also outstanding canoeing (usually open except from September 15-November 15, but check at refuge headquarters; no motorboats). An 18-mile auto tour route from the refuge headquarters to Medicine Lake is open May 1-September 30.

Directions: From Wolf Point, drive east on U.S. 2 for 47 miles to Montana 16. Turn north on Montana 16, which runs through the west end of the refuge. The refuge headquarters is located on the northeast corner of the lake, two miles east of Montana 16.

Ownership: USFWS (789-2305)
Size: 31,457 acres **Closest Town:** Medicine Lake

88   Fox Lake Wildlife Management Area

Description: This is a cattail and bulrush marsh located in an area of scenic rolling hills. It's heavily used by waterfowl (up to 50,000 ducks and geese) and shorebirds both for nesting and for resting during migration. There are five nesting islands built here, and dikes divide the lake into ten independently regulated units. Breeding waterfowl include mallards, pintails, blue- and green-winged teal, shovelers, gadwalls, and redheads. Common shorebirds include American avocets, yellowlegs, willets, upland sandpipers, marbled godwits, and Wilson's phalaropes. Tundra swans and white pelicans commonly visit, and sandhill cranes migrate through, especially in October. Sharp-tailed grouse, gray partridge, pheasants, white-tailed and mule deer, pronghorn antelope, and a variety of raptors can be seen in the upland habitat. Sprague's pipits and burrowing owls also have been seen here. Small boats are permitted in the marsh, and hiking is allowed anywhere; the best walking is along the top of the dikes.

Directions: Take Montana 200 to Lambert, then follow a gravel county road south for a half mile and turn right at the junction of two unnamed county roads. Continue for a little less than a mile to the WMA signs.

Ownership: MDFWP (787-6387)
Size: 1,534 acres **Closest Town:** Lambert

89   Elk Island

Description: This Yellowstone River area of ash and cottonwood trees has an extremely thick underbrush that supports one of the highest densities of white-tailed deer found anywhere in eastern Montana. It's a good spot for birdwatching—one of the most dependable place in the state to see blue jays. It's also a good place to see waterfowl, sharp-tailed grouse, turkeys, and fox squirrels. Beds of freshwater mussels can be found along the river, and raccoons are common. Of particular interest to kids, it's one of the few places in Montana where fireflies can be found. There are no established trails, just follow wildlife paths. A Yellowstone River float trip is also a good way to see wildlife; put in at Intake 16 miles upriver, or put in at Elk Island and float 11.6 miles downriver to Seven Sisters Island.

Directions: Take Montana 16 to Savage, then continue north for one mile. Turn onto a county road and proceed east for two miles.

Ownership: BLM, MDFWP (232-4365)
Size: 1,338 acres
Closest Town: Savage

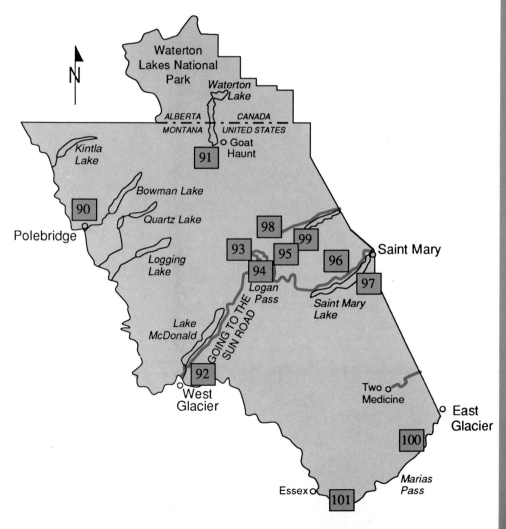

90 **Big Prairie**

Description: This very remote corner of the Park is a large sagebrush and bunchgrass meadow surrounded by spruce and fir forests. It's important winter range for elk and white-tailed deer. A Rocky Mountain wolf population that's rebuilding in this region sometimes utilizes this area; while wolf sightings are rare, their tracks are often visible and their howls are sometimes heard. During the winter, it's an easy six-mile ski trip from the Polebridge Ranger Station to the edge of the meadow and back (ski on the inside North Fork Road). Winter is a stressful time for wildlife, so view from a distance. For a slightly longer trip, continue 4.3 miles north to Round Prairie where deer and elk usually are visible. In the summer, a drive into the meadows offers an opportunity to see deer, coyotes, and assorted songbirds.

Directions: In the summer take the unpaved inside North Fork Road three miles north of Polebridge to Big Prairie. In the winter take the outside North Fork Road to the Polebridge Ranger Station and cross-country ski six miles (roundtrip) to Big Prairie.

Size: 2,600 acres

91 **Kootenai Lakes**

Description: The infrequently visited Goat Haunt area is noted for its spectacular scenery. The trail to Kootenai Lakes, a group of several small lakes surrounded by marshland, meanders through a deep spruce, fir, and pine forest. It is an outstanding place to look for moose. Waterfowl (goldeneyes and mergansers) also inhabit this lush area. While the trail ends at the Kootenai Lakes backpack campsite, unmaintained trails surround the lakes.

Directions: Take the boat from Waterton townsite (located in Waterton Lakes National Park, Canada) to Goat Haunt, Montana, then hike five miles (roundtrip) on the Fifty Mountain Trail to Kootenai Lakes. This area is accessible in summer only.

Size: 49 acres

The dipper, also known as the water ouzel, feeds on insects in shallow, fast-flowing streams. It gets its name from its nearly constant bobbing, or dipping.
MICHAEL S. SAMPLE

92 | **West Glacier Winter Range**

Description: This area on the Park's southern boundary along U.S. 2 is the site of an old burn where elk, white-tailed deer, and mule deer congregate. The best viewing time is late fall through winter on the south-facing slopes. An occasional coyote can be spotted and bald eagles can sometimes be seen along the Middle Fork of the Flathead River; binoculars or spotting scopes are recommended. A trail on the Park side of the river (reached by crossing the old bridge near West Glacier) is a nice two- to three-mile walk or cross-country ski trip into the winter range. Winter is a stressful time for wildlife, so view from a distance.

Directions: From West Glacier, drive approximately three miles east and watch for winter range viewing signs.

Size: 8,500 acres **P**

The Rocky Mountain gray wolf started making a comeback in Montana during the 1980s. It now exists in small numbers in Glacier National Park and the Bob Marshall Wilderness. WILLIAM MUNOZ

Mountain goats are frequently seen by hikers on the Hidden Lake Trail from Logan Pass. This billy surveys its rocky domain above Hidden Lake. MICHAEL S. SAMPLE

93 Going-to-the-Sun Road

Description: This road has numerous parking areas that provide ample wildlife viewing opportunities. Blue grouse often strut on the retaining walls, bald and golden eagles soar overhead, while bear, deer, and mountain goats forage on the slopes. Look for goats near rocky outcroppings, bears in the avalanche chutes, and deer on the grassy slopes. Spectacular wildflower displays vary with the season. Beargrass covers the mountainsides in mid-July through early August, and is a favorite food of elk; mountain goats also favor the leaves, which remain throughout the winter. September is a good time to enjoy colorful fall foliage and look for bears foraging for snowberries. The road is usually open from June through late fall.

Directions: Enter the Park from West Glacier and drive 22 miles to the upper stretches of Going-to-the-Sun Road. This is a ten-mile drive route from the Loop to Logan Pass.

Size: Ten miles

94 Logan Pass Boardwalk

Description: This popular boardwalk wanders through very fragile alpine habitat with spectacular wildflower displays (glacier lilies, beargrass, American bistort, Indian paintbrush). It's one of the nation's only places where ptarmigan (a member of the grouse family that turns from mottled black and white in summer to solid white in winter) can be seen with regularity. Other alpine birds here include grey-crowned rosy finches, mountain bluebirds, and Townsend's solitaires. The boardwalk is also a good place to see hoary marmots. Mountain goats are often seen near the Hidden Lake Overlook, where grizzly bears also can often be viewed from a safe distance, especially in July and August. Do not leave the boardwalk, which is designed to preserve and protect the fragile alpine meadow. It's open June through September, weather permitting.

Directions: Drive to the Logan Pass Visitor Center at the summit of Going-to-the-Sun Road. The 1.5-mile trail begins here and climbs 460 vertical feet.

Size: 1.5 miles **P$**

  There's no other animal quite like the mountain goat in North America. It's closest relative is the chamois of Europe.

GLACIER NATIONAL PARK

95	**Highline Trek**

Description: This 7.6-mile route to Granite Park Chalet provides an outstanding panorama of the Park. In the high alpine meadows, watch bighorn sheep, marmots, and mountain goats at close range. The goats and sheep are often first seen on the mountainsides three miles into the trail near Haystack Butte. Rosy finches, golden eagles, mountain bluebirds, and water pipits also can be seen along the way. The Granite Park Chalet terrace is one of the continent's best places to safely view grizzly bears; it overlooks the spectacular Bear Valley, which is heavily used by grizzlies and closed to humans. A ranger with a spotting scope can usually be found at the chalet in the evenings. Mule deer wander nearby, and golden eagles and pika are occasionally seen. Overnight accomodations and meals at the chalet are by reservation only.

Directions: The trail begins at the Logan Pass Visitor Center. Cross Going-to-the-Sun Road and follow along the Continental Divide (heading northwest) high above the road for 7.6 miles to Granite Park Chalet.

Size: 7.6 miles

96	**Two Dog Flats**

Description: Spring and early summer wildflowers (Indian paintbrush, lupine, blanketflower) are abundant in this open prairie. Visitors may see prairie falcons and other raptors, a variety of songbirds (white-crowned sparrows, MacGillivray's warblers), ground squirrels, and coyotes. Listen for bugling elk in the fall, and view hundreds of elk on the meadows in the winter. Since the road is closed in the winter, this area is good for cross-country skiing (snow permitting) or walking. While there are no trails in this area, hiking is unrestricted.

Directions: From the St. Mary Visitor Center, travel four miles west along Going-to-the-Sun Road.

Size: 500 acres P$

Glacier National Park is one of the best places to see a white-tailed ptarmigan, a bird of high peaks and alpine tundra.
MICHAEL S. SAMPLE

97 | **Red Eagle Valley**

Description: The trail to Red Eagle Lake passes through coniferous forest, open grassland, and aspen and cottonwood groves—excellent for birding, whether you walk a mile or all the way to the lake. The cottonwood groves and open grasslands are a good place to see chipping sparrows, yellow warblers, Swainson's thrushes, and red-naped sapsuckers. The mountain meadows and old-growth spruce forests are good spots to look for northern three-toed woodpeckers, tree swallows, and golden-crowned kinglets. Beaver inhabit the ponds near brushy areas. Those who hike all the way to Red Eagle Lake may see a common loon there. Red Eagle Mountain is a good place to view mountain goats; use your binoculars. This trail is also good for cross-country skiing when there's snow; the designated ski loops are within three miles of the trailhead and travel through elk winter range. While mountain lions are rarely seen, their tracks can often be found here.

Directions: In St. Mary, go to the 1913 Ranger Station where the Red Eagle Trailhead begins. Hike seven miles to Red Eagle Lake.

Size: Seven miles

98 | **Many Glacier**

Description: Wildlife is abundant in the Many Glacier area. On the drive in, view bald and golden eagles along Sherburne Reservoir. Look for bears and coyotes in the aspen groves; listen for common loons and bugling elk in the fall. A number of hiking trails here lead to high-country lakes and glaciers where wildlife can be seen. Mountain goats are common on Grinnell Point, while bighorn sheep are often seen near Ptarmigan Lake. Grizzly bears are often sighted on the treeless slopes above Many Glacier. In November, bighorn sheep move to lower elevations and are often visible near the road, which is often plowed in the winter (check with the Park for current conditions). Cross-country skiers here have a good chance of seeing bighorn sheep and deer.

Directions: Take U.S. 89 to Babb, then drive five miles west to the Park entrance at Many Glacier.

Size: 64,000 acres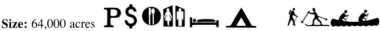

 Montana's largest carnivore is the grizzly bear, which can weigh as much as one thousand pounds. The smallest meat-eater is the pygmy shrew. It weighs less than one-seventh of an ounce.

99 **Cracker Lake Trail**

Description: This trail passes through aspen stands, conifers, open grasslands, and old-growth forests that support a variety of wildlife. Make some noise while you walk, as this area is heavily used by grizzly bears, whose tracks are often seen on the trail. Rufous and calliope hummingbirds and sharp-shinned hawks can be found along the trail, as well as an occasional prairie falcon and golden eagle. Hoary marmots and ground squirrels are common. The steep slopes of Allen Mountain near the lake are a very good place to see bighorn sheep and mountain goats (use binoculars).

Directions: From Babb, drive five miles west to Many Glacier. The trailhead begins at the Many Glacier Hotel parking lot.

Size: Six miles

100 **Firebrand Pass Trail**

Description: This area of prairie potholes is surrounded by grasslands, aspens, and conifers. It's a great birding spot, especially in the spring and fall. Commonly seen birds here include black-capped and mountain chickadees, ruby-crowned kinglets, common snipe, spotted sandpipers, red-tailed hawks, northern harriers, and flickers. Mallards, cinnamon and blue-winged teal, lesser scaup, and American widgeon are often seen in the ponds. The potholes are also a good place to watch beaver.

Directions: Take U.S. 2 to East Glacier, then drive six miles west and park at the Firebrand Pass Trailhead. Follow the trail for 1/4 mile to the beaver ponds.

Size: 1/2 mile **P**

101 **Walton Goat Lick Overlook**

Description: This beautiful area is a great place to see mountain goats. The best goat viewing is from April through mid-July at the licks (natural mineral-laden cliffs) immediately adjacent to the Middle Fork of the Flathead River. As many as 70 goats have been observed at the licks at one time, sometimes aggressively competing for the best licking area. Deer and elk, while not nearly as common, will visit the licks both in spring and fall. The observation area is close to the parking lot.

Directions: Take U.S. 2 to about two miles southeast of Essex. The overlook is immediately adjacent to the road.

Size: 200 acres **P**

102 **Seven Mile Bridge**
103 **Willow Park**
104 **Gardner Canyon**
105 **Blacktail Ponds**
106 **Lamar Valley**
107 **Antelope Creek**
108 **Mount Washburn**
109 **Grand Canyon of the Yellowstone**
110 **Hayden Valley**
111 **LeHardy Rapids**
112 **Fishing Bridge**
113 **Yellowstone Lake**

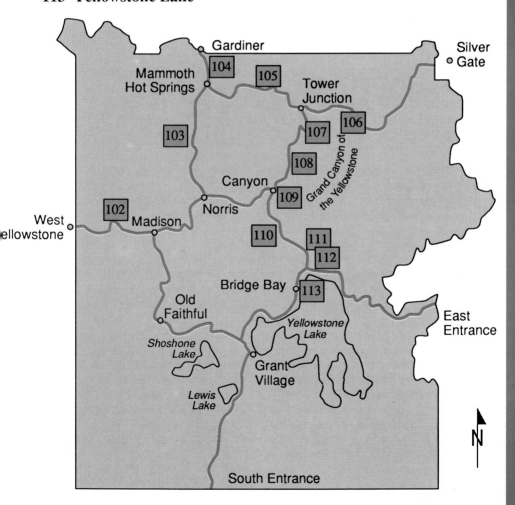

102 Seven Mile Bridge

Description: This is a spectacular area for watching trumpeter swans, which nest in the vicinity; listen for their low-pitched trumpetlike call. Mallards, green-winged teal, and Canada geese can often be found here. Look for bison along the Madison River, and elk can be heard bugling and seen mating in the fall.

Directions: *The bridge is halfway between Madison Junction and West Yellowstone.*

P$

103 Willow Park

Description: This is great moose country in the summer; watch for moose browsing on the willows, especially in the early mornings. The moose are seldom seen in the winter, when they head for the timber and high ridges. The willow stands along Obsidian Creek provide good habitat for a variety of songbirds—Wilson's warblers, yellow warblers, Lincoln's sparrows, and yellowthroat. In the pine forest look for yellow-rumped warblers, dark-eyed juncos, and red-breasted nuthatches.

Directions: *From Mammoth Hot Springs, drive about ten miles south (between Apollinaris Spring and Indian Creek Campground).*

P ⩲ 🏛 ▲ $

104 Gardner Canyon

Description: This canyon is an excellent place to see bighorn sheep, mule deer, and elk in the fall and winter and pronghorn antelope in the summer. It is also one of the best places in the park to look for colorful songbirds including lazuli buntings, western tanagers, and green-tailed towhees. Winter bighorn sheep viewing is exceptional at McMinn Bench; the area is closed during early December to protect breeding sheep. Also in the winter, watch for Townsend's solitaires and look for dippers bobbing up and down on midstream rocks in the Gardner River. In the summer, watch for golden eagles, red-tailed hawks, American kestrels, and prairie falcons. Cliff swallows make their homes on the surrounding canyon walls.

Directions: *Enter the Park from the north at Gardiner and drive to either the 45th Parallel parking area or the Rescue Creek Bridge parking area.*

P 🏛 $

105 Blacktail Ponds

Description: These ponds come alive with birdlife in the spring. The Blacktail Ponds (four connected ponds that are part of one 8.8-acre lake) are among the first to thaw, attracting red-winged blackbirds and sandhill cranes. Listen for the whinny of soras hidden in the grass, and the winnowing of common snipes overhead. Floating Island Lake, another outstanding birdwatching spot, can be found eight miles east of the Blacktail Ponds.

Directions: The Blacktail Ponds are 6.6 miles east of Mammoth Hot Springs enroute to Tower.

Size: 8.8 acres **P$**

106 Lamar Valley

Description: The expansive landscapes of Lamar Valley are home to huge herds of elk and bison. Thousands of animals winter here; look for bighorn sheep browsing on the slopes of Druid Peak at the junction of Lamar River and Soda Butte Creek, moose near the Park's northeast entrance, and coyotes throughout the area. In spring, grizzly bears, black bears, and coyotes circulate among the elk herds, looking for vulnerable calves. In summer, see mule deer and pronghorn antelope. Golden eagles, prairie falcons, and American kestrels are common. The Lamar River Trail that begins 1.5 miles east of where Soda Butte Creek and Lamar River join is usually good for cross-country skiing.

Directions: Enter the Park from the north (Gardiner) or northeast (near Cooke City). Lamar Valley lies between Tower Junction and the northeast entrance.

Size: 70,000 acres **P⅄$**

The long-tailed weasel can be found in a variety of habitats—forest, grassland, and even desert. In the winter they turn completely white and are commonly called ermine. MICHAEL S. SAMPLE

107 | Antelope Creek

Description: With a good pair of binoculars, a spotting scope, and some patience, this is a reliable place to safely view grizzly bears—one of the best spots in the Park. The best viewing time is right at dawn and probably in June, when the bears are preying on elk calves, although bears can be seen here throughout the summer. Viewing in this bear management area is strictly from the road; several good pullouts offer unobstructed views. Watch bears dig up vegetation, court, and breed. At Calcite Spring Overlook look for bighorn sheep on the ridge east of the road, north of Tower Fall. This valley is also a good area to hear bugling elk in the fall.

Directions: From Tower Junction, drive just a few miles south past Tower Falls.

P⅄$

Grizzly bears are sometimes seen along Antelope Creek in Yellowstone National Park. They are the largest carnivores in Montana, although in fact a Yellowstone grizzly's diet is usually 60 percent plants and only 40 percent meat. Grizzly bears in Yellowstone often prey on elk calves in the spring. TOM MANGELSEN

108 | Mount Washburn

Description: This hike passes through alpine tundra and provides panoramas of wild country. In the summer, bighorn sheep can be seen on Mount Washburn. You may encounter blue grouse on the way up, or red squirrels harvesting whitebark pine cones; the nuts from the cones are a major food of Yellowstone grizzly bears. Noisy Clark's nutcrackers also pick and store the nuts for winter; the seeds they don't find become tomorrow's whitebark pines. Other summer birds here include hairy woodpeckers, Cooper's hawks, golden eagles, peregrine falcons, gray jays, and rosy finches. This is fragile alpine tundra, so please do not leave the trail. The six-mile roundtrip hike takes about three hours and climbs 1,400 vertical feet; be sure to carry water.

Directions: Mount Washburn is accessible via a three-mile hike from two points on the Tower-Canyon road. Either park at the Dunraven Pass picnic area or drive one mile up the old Chittenden Road (four miles north of Dunraven Pass) to a parking area.

Size: Three-mile hike (10,243 feet high)

109 | Grand Canyon of the Yellowstone

Description: This spectacular canyon is a great area for nesting raptors. It's probably the best place in the park to see osprey; as many as seven nesting pairs have been seen in a year and a nest can almost always be spotted (ask a ranger if you can't find one). Look for nesting osprey from mid-June to early July on the canyon's rocky pinnacles. Also watch for kestrels, Clark's nutcrackers, common ravens, and gray jays.

Directions: At Canyon Junction take the North Rim Drive to Grandview and Lookout Point.

P$

Wildlife watching includes small, common animals, such as this least chipmunk. Chipmunks are one of the most common animals seen by visitors to Yellowstone National Park.
MICHAEL S. SAMPLE

101

110 | Hayden Valley

Description: This may well be the Park's most spectacular wildlife area. Look for grizzly bears digging for pocket gophers in the spring and bellowing bison breeding from late July to early August; watch for bison uncovering grass from deep snow with swings of their massive heads in winter. The Alum Creek pullout is a good place to look for shorebirds (long-billed dowitcher, western sandpiper, greater yellowlegs) in the spring and fall, while the Yellowstone River holds white pelicans, trumpeter swans, Canada geese, goldeneyes, and mallards. You may see sandhill cranes and coyotes in the open meadows. This is a great place to listen for bugling elk in the fall.

Directions: Hayden Valley lies between Canyon and Fishing Bridge. There are many pullouts and overlooks.

Size: 18,000 acres **P$**

Bison are the largest land animals in North America, weighing up to 2,000 pounds. The calves usually are born in May. Hayden Valley is one of the best places in Yellowstone to view bison during the summer. MICHAEL S. SAMPLE

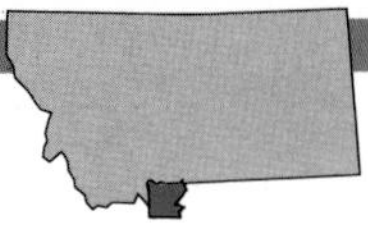

111 | LeHardy Rapids

Description: This is an outstanding area to watch spawning cutthroat trout leap the rapids, then rest in pools just below them, during June and July. The rare harlequin duck is sometimes seen diving into the turbulent water looking for aquatic insects. This is a good spot to see dippers and an occasional otter. Gray jays can be seen in the nearby conifers. Fishing is prohibited 100 yards on either side of the rapids.

Directions: The rapids are halfway between Mud Volcano (south of Canyon Village) and Fishing Bridge.

P$

112 | Fishing Bridge

Description: Watch native cutthroat trout spawn under this bridge in June and July. White pelicans can sometimes be seen catching fish in the shallow waters—swallowing the fish whole—while Barrow's goldeneyes and California gulls are common. Watch for coyotes walking along the shore.

Directions: Fishing Bridge is at the north end of Yellowstone Lake.

P$

113 | Yellowstone Lake

Description: Take a one-hour boat tour around Stevenson Island for an outstanding opportunity to view bald eagles (the island is closed to the public from May 15-August 15 to protect nesting birds). Look for California gulls, buffleheads, and Barrow's goldeneyes near Bridge Bay and watch for gray jays and Clark's nutcrackers in forested areas along the shoreline. This is a large cold lake, so small boats should stay close to shore and stay off the lake during windy weather. Boat tours run from June 4-September 17; the cost is $6 for adults and $3 for children (5-11). Gull Point Drive, just south of Bridge Bay along the shoreline, is a good area to look for belted kingfishers, lesser scaup, buffleheads, common snipe, and spotted sandpipers.

Directions: From Bridge Bay, take a short boat tour around Stevenson Island, or use your own boat.

Size: 91,704 acres **P**

ABOUT DEFENDERS OF WILDLIFE

Defenders of Wildlife is a national, nonprofit conservation organization of more than 80,000 members and supporters dedicated to preserving the natural abundance and diversity of wildlife and its habitat. Defenders has field offices in several locations across the United States, and the national headquarters is in Washington, D.C.

Defenders has been closely involved with developing wildlife viewing guides in several states, including Oregon, Montana, Idaho, and Utah. We anticipate that by the year 2000, Defenders will have assisted most states in the formation of wildlife viewing systems.

Defenders has provided similar leadership on many other conservation issues, including:

- working for improved management of our national wildlife refuge system.
- increasing protection for seals, whales, turtles, and other sea life that are threatened by drift nets or plastic pollution.
- providing direction for California bond initiatives that have resulted in more than $130 million for wildlife habitat acquisition.
- guiding efforts to restore the Rocky Mountain Wolf to Yellowstone National Park.

If you are interested in becoming a member, annual dues are $20, which includes six issues of our bimonthly magazine, *Defenders*. To join or for further information, write or call Defenders of Wildlife, 1244 19th St. N.W., Washington, DC 20036, phone 202-659-9510.

MORE BOOKS FROM FALCON PRESS

Falcon Press publishes a wide variety of outdoor books and calendars, including the state-by-state series of wildlife viewing guides called the Watchable Wildlife Series. If you liked this book, please look for the companion books on other states.

If you want to know more about outdoor recreation in Montana, then look for *The Hiker's Guide to Montana, The Floater's Guide to Montana, The Hiker's Guide to Montana's Continental Divide Trail,* and *Montana National Forests*—all from Falcon Press.

To purchase any of these books, please check with your local bookstore or call toll-free 1-800-582-BOOK. When you call, please ask for a free catalog listing all the fine books and calendars from Falcon Press.

Falcon Press Publishing Co., Inc., P.O. Box 1718, Helena, MT 59624.